Praise for *Holy Hot Mess*

"Mary Katherine Backstrom's words are so immediately engaging, so filled with humor, and so seemingly effortless, that their depth and insight sneak up on you. She has a way of cutting through the flowery facade of religious-speak and allowing us to reach the unvarnished heart of what it is to live as a real human being with an authentic, broken-in faith. This is a beautiful travel guide through the messy places."

—John Pavlovitz, author, pastor, activist

"In *Holy Hot Mess*, Mary Katherine takes us on an unabashed and authentic ride through stories both humorous and heart-wrenching. MK is all at once relatable, witty, and touching. I recommend this book as an example of relentless faith that is relatable and inspiring for all."

—Colin Balfe, founder of Love What Matters

"*Holy Hot Mess* couldn't have come at a more perfect time in my life. I often forget that all of the things happening in my life are for a reason, even if it doesn't make sense at the time. Mary Katherine uses her humor to share hilarious and at times heartbreaking personal stories that remind each of us that there is a beautiful plan unfolding in our lives, and it's bigger and more beautiful than we can fathom. Every heartbreak and obstacle has a purpose, and after reading her book I will surely be switching my perspective and reminding myself that nothing is in my control. Thank you for reminding me that all of us are a hot mess at different points in our lives—some just hide it better than others."

—Tiffany Jenkins

"Mary Katherine Backstrom doesn't sugarcoat, nor does she hold back on the messy truths of her life. It's not because MK doesn't care; it's because she cares so much. Reading this delightful and funny book is a little bit like grabbing coffee and a side of therapy with your slightly sassy Southern best friend who is also best friends with Jesus."

—Jen Mann, *New York Times* bestselling author of *Midlife Bites: Anyone Else Falling Apart, Or Is It Just Me?*

"Life, like my good friend Mary Katherine, can be very messy. However, her heart is pure, and her words give me hope. If you are a member of the hot mess club, you will enjoy this book. Faith and love of the Lord don't have to look polished to be genuine."

—Meredith Masony

"Mary Katherine Backstrom's writing makes every mama want to stand up and shout AMEN!!! She is so authentic and relatable. Every sentence feels like a fun, hilarious, honest chat with your BFF. A BFF who isn't afraid to admit her life is a hot mess! And really, who needs any other kind of friend?"

—Deva Dalporto, @MyLifeSuckers

"Mary Katherine has a way of cutting straight through the pretension and polish to get to the messy middle of life's big questions. As a fellow mother and person of faith trying to navigate all the things, I can't help but nod along with her stories and personal revelations—as well as laugh out loud at the hilarious situations she finds herself in. Anyone seeking solidarity and support in their own imperfect journey will appreciate the raw honesty, relatable humor, and real heart of *Holy Hot Mess*."

—Annie Reneau, associate editor, Upworthy

HOLY
HOT
MESS

HOLY HOT MESS

FINDING GOD *in the* DETAILS
of this WEIRD *and* WONDERFUL LIFE

MARY KATHERINE BACKSTROM

New York • Nashville

Worthy

Hachette Book Group

1290 Avenue of the Americas, New York, NY 10104

worthypublishing.com

twitter.com/worthypub

First Edition: August 2021

Worthy is a division of Hachette Book Group, Inc. The Worthy name and logo are trademarks of Hachette Book Group, Inc.

The publisher is not responsible for websites (or their content) that are not owned by the publisher.

The Hachette Speakers Bureau provides a wide range of authors for speaking events. To find out more, go to www.hachettespeakersbureau.com or call (866) 376-6591.

Print book interior design by Bart Dawson.

Library of Congress Cataloging-in-Publication Data

Names: Backstrom, Mary Katherine, author.

Title: Holy hot mess : finding God in the details of this weird and wonderful life / Mary Katherine Backstrom.

Description: First edition. | Nashville : Worthy, 2021. | Summary: "Mary Katherine Backstrom shares heart-breaking and hilarious stories of how God uses each "mess" in our lives to bring us closer to Him. She shows readers that it's okay to celebrate exactly where they are right now—holy, hot mess and all. A lot of people struggle with the concept of being holy. But the fact is, even the hottest of messes are being shaped—right now—into Jesus' likeness. In this book, Mary Katherine shares the sometimes—hidden evidence of God's work in her life and shows you that it's okay to embrace the hot messes. Holy Hot Mess is separated into three parts: You Are Messy (Identity and Parenting) They Are All a Mess (Love and Friendship) Being a Hot, Holy Mess (Faith) The book will cover all of the topics that plague our hearts every day with raw honest truth with a side of laughter. Mary Katherine invites you into her story as a friend, encouraging you to embrace the hot messes in your life because you are the person God created you to be"—Provided by publisher.

Identifiers: LCCN 2021010630 | ISBN 9781546015499 (hardcover) | ISBN 9781546015505 (ebook)

Subjects: LCSH: Backstrom, Mary Katherine. | Christian biography—United States.

Classification: LCC BR1725. B28 A3 2021 | DDC 270.092 [B]—dc23

LC record available at https://lccn.loc.gov/2021010630

Printed in the United States of America

LSC-C

Printing 1, 2021

To Daddy, who taught me the life-changing lesson that there's strength in owning your mess.

CONTENTS

FOREWORD

A memory popped up on my social media recently of Mary Katherine and me in the bathroom stall of a nice restaurant, wrapped up like mummies in cheap toilet paper, contorting our facial muscles into our best attempt at model expressions until my cheeks literally hurt, and taking selfies. There is a story behind that mess, but more on that later…

First, let's start with this: I love a good mess. Messes are unpretentious. They're relatable. They're full of life. They're a great reminder of our humanity.

Somewhere between the time I started creating videos on social media, and my small hobby exploding into something bigger than I ever expected, I was advised that my creative outlet was now an *actual* career (as if I'm a grown-up or something) and for legal/business/boring purposes, I needed to create an s-corporation. I spent some time researching names of other similar corporations, and I noticed a trend emerge. Many of these corporations were named after a single, meaningful word that represented superiority. So I decided to use a single, meaningful word as well: Flawed. The name of my s-corp would serve as a reminder that I am never to waste my time chasing perfection and that being flawed doesn't make me inadequate. Our flaws simply make us human.

I often say that I'm thankful social media didn't exist back when I was at my rock bottom, struggling as a newly divorced, depressed, and seriously broke mom. So much of social media just leaves people feeling "less than." And though this trend has been changing recently (humans are finally willing to be more *human* in their posts), Mary Katherine was one of the first people I noticed on social media who exuded authenticity.

Boy, was that refreshing. Seeing authenticity on social media feels like a tall glass of homemade lemonade on a scorching hot day. Or peeing alone in private when you're a mother of young kids. Or your teenager saying, "Mom, you're doing an excellent job parenting. How can I help around the house today?" and wanting nothing in return! But I digress...

I didn't know MK personally, but I had seen a few of her posts on Facebook. I think maybe we met once briefly at a conference, but most of my brain cells, including the ones linked to memory, have been destroyed by motherhood, so I might be making that up.

A few years after I first saw MK on my timeline, she was in Los Angeles for an appearance on the Ellen DeGeneres show. After seeing one of MK's videos, Ellen herself fell in love with MK's authenticity, storytelling, and her infectious laugh.

It's kind of hard not to.

Since I live in the outskirts of LA, Mary Katherine and I decided to meet up for dinner. It felt like having a meal with an old friend, the kind of friend I had known for years, shared awkward memories and had probably gotten into some trouble with.

Before our toilet paper selfies, we first dined like somewhat-classy people. We bonded over our love of carbs, our completely different and yet somehow relatable childhoods, our spiritual beliefs, and our passion for helping humans be kinder to themselves. We talked about the small stuff and the really, really hard stuff, laughing and crying (occasionally simultaneously) over the unbelievable highs and heartbreaking lows life had thrown our way.

And that's when I realized something.

MK and KK are a mess!

A big. Huge. Mess.

And so are you, the person reading this.

You're a mess.

Some messes are of our own making because we are flawed (yet wonderful) humans. Often, we make those messes much messier by piling on a whole bunch of unnecessary stress because we refuse to give ourselves an ounce of grace.

And then there are the messes that are completely out of our control. The ones that are thrown in our faces unexpectedly and stop our whole world. Sometimes for a moment. Sometimes for years.

As you'll find out reading this book, Mary Katherine has walked through some terrifying messes. And I'm sure you have as well.

The way I see it, there are three ways that us humans deal with the mess.

One: Pretend there is no mess. Denial. Go through the motions. Live without fully being alive. Not allowing yourself to really feel the hard stuff.

I tried that, and nah, not for me.

Two: Exhaust yourself trying to clean up the mess and make it all perfect, even if it means sacrificing everything that matters (including your sanity) in the process.

Tried that too, and nah, not for me.

Three: Throw yourself in the mess. Dig into the most uncomfortable corners of your existence. Address the stuffiest of stuffs, cry it out, scream it out, and ask for help. And sometimes (read: often) you'll find some life-changing lessons and even some *beauty* in that mess.

I tried that, and yup, that's for me. And those kinds of people are my kind of people.

Mary Katherine is my people.

This is exactly what *Holy Hot Mess* is about.

MK's vulnerability, her unique perspective, and her beautiful way with words will help you feel seen, and help your own mess feel a little bit more manageable. In a world that constantly pushes you toward chasing perfection (unattainable), MK will encourage you to embrace the mess (trust me, definitely attainable!).

And, the best part? You'll feel like you're having a meal with an old friend who understands, who won't judge you, who's been there and who can hold your hand through it. Maybe even finish the evening in a bathroom stall, taking selfies. Just don't hurt your face.

—Kristina Kuzmič, author of *Hold On, But Don't Hold Still*

INTRODUCTION

For I am confident of this very thing, that He who
began a good work in you will perfect it until the day
of Christ Jesus.

—Philippians 1:6 NASB 1995

It's two o'clock in the morning, and a pot of coffee is brewing.
If I were a doctor or heading to the gym, maybe this would
make more sense. But I am not a doctor, and I hate working out.
I'm a slightly fluffy, exhausted mother of two who looks forward
to bed all day.

I. Love. Sleep.

Yet, sleep is no longer an option this morning. I'm awake
with an itch in my heart that's impossible to ignore. Whether
it's something stirring in my soul or simply an anxiety attack, it's
hard to say. Whatever it is, I'm gonna chase it.

So, I pour myself a cup of coffee and step out onto my porch.
Crickets are chirping and automatic sprinklers are dancing, but
the rest of the world is still. The air is so quiet that for the first
time this week, I can actually hear my own thoughts.

Turns out, it isn't anxiety that has pulled me out of the bed. It's something else entirely. It's revelation. I've spent months wrestling over this manuscript, struggling to get it *just right*. And after all that struggle, I'm awake this morning with an invariable sense of clarity.

I know what I'm trying to say!

Never mind this book is due in a month or that I'm stuck halfway through the manuscript. Here I am in the pitch dark, with a mind full of words, and that deadline no longer scares me. I have a full pot of coffee and an arrow in my heart pointing the way I should go. Anxiety has relinquished the steering wheel.

Finally, I'm back in control.

I crack my knuckles and open a Word doc. The cursor blinks, full of potential. The words are coming to me fast. I stretch my fingers over the keyboard, and then…there's a creak at the door.

"Mommy?" a tiny voice beckons me. "Mommy, I need you—*quick*! My toot fell out on my pillow!"

Skkkkkrrrrrt.

There's something you need to know: In our family, *fart* is the f-word. This isn't a rule my husband and I created. It was instituted by the kids' grandparents. Bless them, they are sensitive that way. So, to replace the horribly offensive f-word, we adopted a fart replacement: *toot*. That being said, if a toot *fell* out on my daughter's pillow, we have a very serious problem.

I close my laptop and follow her down the hall.

What was it I wanted to write about?

• • • • • • •

INTRODUCTION

I know you. I really feel like I do. You're juggling all the things: the kids, the house, the dreams of what life could be, the realities of the bank account. You know there's got to be more out there and that you're not just here by some random universal chemical spill. But it's hard to imagine what kind of intention could possibly be out there, given the messy way life rolls out. In many ways, you are living the dream. But you're surprised it doesn't feel weightier. Some days, those things you chased for so long feel hollow in your hands.

You thought you'd have it more together by now. That you'd be more adulty. That you would plan your meals and follow the stock market. That your steps would feel more steady. You figured by now that surely you would make your bed in the mornings. But no, that's not your life.

Instead, you make big plans and they change. You envision a brighter tomorrow, and then you wake up with a nasty case of pinkeye. You download a meditation and prayer app in an attempt to build your spirituality. But you turn it on, lie down in bed, and it makes you fall asleep.

Oops.

That's how I can know you, and you me. We're in this mess together. It's like we blinked, and all of a sudden became the adult in the room. And I don't know about you, but I have a serious case of imposter syndrome…

I swear it was just yesterday that I was a baby-faced college kid dating a shaggy-haired soccer player named Ian. He was pre-med and I was pre-dropout, but we believed we had *everything* in common. (Love is a helluva drug, y'all.)

Fifteen years later, we share the same last name and a whole

3

lot of other things, too. A boatload of student debt, two beautiful children, and a home that is chock-full of creatures. We have a son named Ben, a daughter named Holland, and two terribly behaved dogs. Oh, and a scraggeldy cat that we found in the Waffle House parking lot, whom my son aptly named Waffles. Ian finished his training, and I am an author now. But if you were to ask me how any of this happened, I would tell you: I don't have a clue.

My plan was to be a rock star or an astronaut, maybe get a few elementary schools named after me, then marry Prince William and retire as a princess. But God made Kate Middleton, so here I am, editing a manuscript on a sticky kitchen table while the kids yell: "*Mommmmm*—I'm huuuuungry!"

Children are the ultimate Needers of Things. I'm perpetually answering their calls. In the last ten minutes, I have wiped two bottoms, cleaned up a spill, and logged into a first-grade Zoom class. And now they want me to feed them…again.

What do these kids think I am, a *grown-up*?

There's no way I am one of those. Grown-ups know all of the things. About marriage, finances, and parenting. Grown-ups know how to replace a flat tire and cook a decent turkey for Thanksgiving. As a child, I believed grown-ups had all of the answers but here I am at thirty-six, and the strangest thing keeps happening: I keep collecting more questions. About friendship, and faith, and finances. About marriage and my purpose in this world.

I don't have all the answers. I don't know anyone who does! It feels like we are just out in this world, looking for a thread that ties all of this randomness together. Some proof of intention that points to a higher purpose and gives meaning to our chaos and mess.

Are you with me? Good. Let's go on a journey. Let's chase down that thread, together. Let's stare down the messy places in our lives, until something divine shines through. I believe there's a voice in each of our lives that is struggling to gain our attention. It is loudest in moments when life stands still, when we are forced to reckon with silence. We aren't really sure that we want to hear it, so we busy ourselves with life. But the whisper remains, and it tugs at our hearts. I hear it, and I believe you do, too.

Its message echoes in the rafters of our minds, whispering, "There's something more."

• • • • • • •

It was a little while back, at some kitschy beach shop, my daughter Holland (yes, she of the fallen toot) fell in love with a necklace. Actually, it was more of a statement piece. It had a hand-sized plastic tusk that "belonged" to a saber-toothed tiger. "Saber-toothed tiger necklace charm" would not do this thing justice. It's a veritable paleolithic medallion, assuming saber-tooths are from that dinosaur era. Yesterday, she pulled that tooth off her necklace and tucked it into her braid.

"I'm a *caveman*!" she yelled, before jumping off the couch and stripping down to her panties. And she was, y'all. Completely freaking feral. She kept this character for the rest of the day, grunting as I tucked her in to bed. And then sometime around three a.m., that tooth fell out of her braid. And *this*, folks, is what has driven her out of bed during what is supposed to be my writer's nirvana, looking for Mommy's assistance.

"My toot!" she says, pointing to the tusk. "Can you put it back in my hair?"

Part of me is frustrated. There will be no writing this morning. But I'm also relieved. At least it wasn't the turd I was expecting.

"Sure, honey," I reply, releasing a chest-deep sigh. "Then go back to sleep. Please?"

You probably know as well as I do that that's not going to happen.

Isn't this just how life is sometimes? It's like you are on a trapeze. One moment, you're swinging into work, ascending as fast as you can. Momentum is building, you reach the pinnacle, and—*gasp*—you're suspended in air and time. The world shifts clearly into view. Then something (a phone call, a missing toot, a nasty comment, whatever life throws your way) pulls you in the opposite direction. Falling backward, the view is blurry again. You're stuck between two worlds, again. Is it possible to fully exist in either one?

The sun is rising over Florida now, and my daughter will not go back to sleep. I won't get any writing done today. Turns out, that steering wheel I thought I could grasp before dawn was just an illusion. The truth is, I'm not in control of this ride. Perhaps I never have been. The trapeze of life has pulled me away from my job. So, instead of meeting an important deadline, I will be doing the work of a mother: curled up on the couch, reading *Pete the Cat*, snuggling my brown-eyed girl.

I could never regret such a precious moment, but I do have some questions for God. *Like…Hey, God. If You do have a plan for my life, could you make it a little bit easier? And if You want me to go in a different direction, could I at least have some sort of sign? Will my hands ever grip the steering wheel? Will I ever have any control? I'm cool with You driving—You're God, after all. But honestly...where are we going?*

This isn't a book that answers those questions. If that's what you're looking for, sorry. The deal is, I'm still flying on this trapeze. What this book *is* about is truth telling. It's about the truth that God's shaping of us doesn't stop once we become "grown-ups." It's about the truth that church (as we seem to define it) doesn't have all the answers. It's about the truth that people are going to let us down and we them, and yet we still need people. And that none of these truths have to keep us twisted up, thinking that out there, somewhere, is a place where mess doesn't happen. It's about learning to live fully in the duality that exists in both the mountaintops of clarity and the marshes of the mess.

You see, mess doesn't cancel out the marvelous. And the Creator of the marvelous chooses not to cancel out the mess. These pages are filled with as many questions as answers, but the thing is, that's *real* life. We aren't born with a road map, and even if we were, who the heck uses road maps anymore? What we really want when we get a little lost is to say "Hey, Siri! Show me the way." And a little omniscient voice would respond with step-by-step directions: *This is the job that you're supposed to work. That's the person you're supposed to marry. This is how many children you'll have. This is the way you should vote.*

But that's not how any of this works. God doesn't live in our phones. We don't get to ping Him and receive audible answers (though that would be freaking amazing). No, we are all down here together on earth, figuring things out as we go. Living and learning by making mistakes. Flying by the seat of our pants.

Sometimes the lessons we learn are hilarious. Sometimes they hurt like hell. I can attest; I've experienced both. But let me tell you, there is beauty in the chaos. Looking back on life's messiest moments, I now see the fingerprints of God.

Life is like a puzzle spread out on a table, and we don't get to see the picture from the box. Heck, most of us are just wondering if there even *is* a picture. We feel stress and confusion over our scattered pieces. But that's normal. It's the nature of who we are.

We are active construction sites, all mess and mud. We are artworks in progress, with paint on the floor. We don't have a clue where this thing is going. But listen to me: God *does*.

There is a picture on your puzzle box. Not only that, but He's the one who painted it. And those life moments that make you cringe, or cry, or laugh uncomfortably? They are part of that picture, too.

In this book, I share some of my life's messiest moments. And how looking back, I now recognize a holy undercurrent beneath the chaos. What I hope for your life is that as you read, you begin to sort through your own messes and an overall picture will begin to emerge. A powerful connection to something greater, one you haven't even realized was there. A story that has all the elements of a great book: the highs and the lows, and the unexpected. Suspense, heartbreak, and joy. A common thread that ties it all together. One puzzle piece connecting to another.

Proof that God is still at work in the thick of our biggest messes.

CHAPTER 1

CHECK UNDER THE CAR SEAT

Have no fear of perfection—you'll never reach it.

—Salvador Dalí

I've always considered myself a truth teller. Pretty much. Generally speaking. Usually.

There *was* that one time as a kid when I stole a pair of socks from the store at my weekly gymnastics lesson. You see, my family was poor, and my socks looked like cotton Swiss cheese. Which wasn't great, because all I wanted in the whole wide world was to catch the eye of a twelve-year-old boy in my Wednesday night tumbling class. He had blue eyes and swoopy blond hair, and y'all, he could do a back handspring! Not only that, but his adult teeth had all come in perfectly straight, and he went to a middle school across town, which was so very exotic in the eyes of a small-town fifth grade girl.

As if all of that wasn't too much for my eleven-year-old heart to bear, get this: His name was Swift. Freaking *Swift*. That kid was bred to be a heartthrob. His parents knew what they were doing. It was like they had a conference in the delivery room and said, "What other James Dean–esque name could possibly befit a sexy-maverick-artist-gymnast? With great hair?" And Swift became the obvious winner.

Clearly, I had to win his love, but that wasn't going to be possible with my ratty, hand-me-down, too-big socks.

One day, at the beginning of class, I asked my coach for a sip of water. On the way to the fountain, I slipped into the leotard store and found the most brilliant pair of white socks that you ever did see. I couldn't afford them, but I had to have them.

And so, well...I stole them.

I shoved those socks down the front of my leotard and bee-lined for the girls' locker room. Then, safely hidden inside the walls of a beige bathroom stall, I ripped the tags off of those puppies and pulled them over my feet.

They were so crisp. So thick. So very hole-free. I wiggled my toes with pleasure and grinned. Then I flushed every bit of evidence down the locker room commode.

You can probably imagine what happened next. It wasn't my best moment, I have to admit. I scrambled out of the bathroom stall as the toilet belched unholy liquids all over the floor behind me. I'd hoped to scurry away unnoticed, but the next class of preteen girls were already at their lockers, changing clothes. They were screeching and pointing in my general direction. They completely ruined my getaway. I was cold freaking busted. My perfect heist resulted in a soggy pile of shame.

Next thing I knew, adults were circled around me, looking down their noses at my thieving, lying face. They were wagging their fingers and muttering words like *horrible* and *ungrateful* and *disappointing*. Their voices blended together like a hot smoothie of shame, dumped over the top of my head. I wanted to disappear, but I couldn't. The shaming was relentless. With all of my peers watching in horror, Coach called Roto-Rooter and asked for my momma's number.

My mother. Oh God, she's gonna kill me!

The plumber fished my sad little socks from the septic catacombs beneath our gym as I sat in the lobby, awaiting my death. The gym owner was furious. She insisted the evidence be placed inside a Ziploc bag. Exhibit A in my prosecution.

When Momma finally arrived, I was publicly convicted. And to amplify my horror, Swift sat there the entire time, crisscross applesauce, watching the whole fiasco. His eyes wide in horror. Swoopy bangs and all.

Walking the Green Mile to my mom's minivan, the air was so thick you could spread it over toast. I fixed my eyes on the floorboard as I buckled my seat belt. Momma turned the ignition and our favorite song, "Love Shack," came blaring through the radio. The two of us had a tradition of rolling the windows down and screaming out every lyric together. But in that moment, she smashed the Off button so hard and fast that I was afraid it would be stuck that way forever.

"We will talk about this when we get home," she said. She added a heavy sigh in case I wasn't already convinced how sad she was to have birthed me.

Anyways, back to truth telling.

I've tried to make it my thing ever since. In my experience, lies only snowball (or clog up toilets), whereas the truth just handles things with brutal efficiency. The bottom line is, whatever you purchase with a lie will come back with a tab of compounding interest. Take it from me: A single lie derailed my Olympic gymnastics dreams, ended my star-crossed love with Swift, and cost my mother three hundred dollars…all in a matter of an hour. I had tried not to pay for that fresh new pair of socks, but the plumbing repair could have bought numerous packs.

Later that evening I sat in bed, eyes swollen with tears. Momma walked into my room and quietly sat beside me. Then, she pulled me deep into a much-needed hug. She didn't force me to relive my shame. She didn't ask me if my lie was worth it. We both knew that it wasn't. Instead, Momma saw through my disastrous exterior and straight into the heart of a child. I only wanted to feel seen and loved. By hugging me close, in my most vulnerable moment, she let me know that I already was.

I was in fifth grade when I learned that the truth can be an uncomfortable friend. Life is hard, and sometimes owning our imperfect reality can feel like a stab in the heart. But at least when truth hurts, the injury is clean and quick. On the flip side, lies are made of jagged edges. The wounds they cause are messy and not so easily healed.

• • • • • • •

Now, I don't know if you've ever watched a makeup tutorial on YouTube, but holy smokes those things are amazing. In a matter of minutes, even the plainest face can be masterfully transformed into, well, literally anything else. I am dead serious, y'all! I have seen a fourteen-year-old girl go from Jeremy Renner to Kylie Jenner using some modern voodoo magic that kids these days call *contouring*.

Contouring is the most smoke-and-mirrors makeup trick ever. It literally uses tints and shadows to redirect light on your face. Your nose can look smaller, your forehead shorter, or whatever else your body-morphing heart desires, all without injections or scalpels involved. Kudos to the drag queen scientist who created this incredible magic. They've got every one of us plainlings walking around looking like Calvin Klein models.

And...I ain't mad about it.

But.

I have to point out that this deceiving concept isn't exactly novel. People are shifty creatures, like I've told you, and we've been testing our truth-bending skills since that whole apple-in-the-Garden episode that left women with the curse of painful childbirth and ridiculous-looking leaf clothes.

What I'm getting at here is that human beings are a lying bunch of tricksters, and we start honing these skills from the moment we are in Pampers. Don't believe me? I present to you my children, who by the ripe age of four had already learned that there are special types of lies to use in different situations.

For instance:

Have you ever seen a chocolate-faced kid look directly into the eyes of their mother and outright deny that they snuck a bite of cake? That's a *bald-faced lie*.

Have you ever seen a one-year-old hide behind a curtain, clearly trying to poop their pants, and when you ask them what they are doing, they simply refuse to answer? That's a *lie of omission.*

Has a child ever come running up to you, confessing that the cat is soaking wet but neglecting to mention the fact that they dumped their apple juice all over the poor creature? That's a *"half-truth" lie.*

(Note: Yes, my kids did every one of these things. Raising truth tellers is an exhausting affair, y'all. I'm working uphill against sin nature.)

Now, I'm going to give your parents the benefit of the doubt and assume you were raised to know better than stealing socks, pouring juice on the family cat, or flirting with your neighbor's husband. That is some entry-level morality stuff, and even the hottest messes among us know better.

But there's an entirely new type of lie that was born in our generation, and I think it's important that we talk about how to fight it. This lie puts a new spin on some old classics, but with a little more YouTube makeup flair.

The newest trick that Satan has unleashed upon this world is what I'm going to call the Lie of Curation. This lie is an Insta-worthy, truth-contouring mastermind. You feed your messy life into those filters—and *boop!*—out pops a picture-perfect, postable version.

If you've ever tried scrolling through Instagram, you know what I'm talking about. The Lie of Curation is a highly edited, filtered, and fancified version of the truth. And the danger of the Lie of Curation is that it doesn't immediately dole out a painful consequence.

When you flush a sock down the toilet, a consequence gurgles right up, but the Lie of Curation just continues to survive—as long as you are willing to nurture it.

And whoa, are folks willing to nurture it. A 2018 Nielsen study revealed that American adults spend eleven hours a day immersed in various media and scrolling through curated newsfeeds.

Eleven. Hours.

Do I even need to unpack what this is doing for our emotional, mental, and spiritual health?

How is a soul supposed to flourish when we spend the majority of our waking hours immersed in a world where everything messy is edited out and everything pretty is enhanced? It's an odd phenomenon, this social media thing. Because at the root of it all, we are just showing up, putting the most beautiful versions of ourselves on display, and hoping to find real community and love. What's happening is quite the opposite.

When we hide our messy, authentic selves from people, we are never truly seen. Instead, we invest so much time in this bizarre world that we buy into the lie that it is real.

So often within the Lie of Curation, there are things presented as "raw" or "real" or "transparent" or "messy." But even those things are carefully crafted for the sake of being "relatable." Can we acknowledge how bizarre this is? That folks are pouring so much energy into appearing messy and relatable rather than embracing the mess that exists in their lives and, I dunno, actually *being* relatable?

The truth is, we're all guilty of participating in this Lie of

Curation that prevents authentic community from taking place. We've tethered ourselves to a phantom post, as if there's joy to be found there. And then we act baffled as to why we feel like half-deflated balloons fluttering in the wind.

· · · · · · ·

Last week I called my friend Melissa to see if she had time for a lunch date. It had been a while since we caught up, and I was missing my friend. A little bit about Melissa: She is a brilliant doctor and a loving mother. She works out every day, her kids love vegetables, and her car smells like it was bought yesterday. Honestly, it's just a bit intimidating, but she loves me well, so I tolerate her amazingness as much as I can. Turned out, Melissa was available for lunch, and so was her husband, Eliot. I planned to third-wheel-it to our favorite local seafood joint to catch up and have some adult time. They pulled up in my driveway and honked the horn, and I hopped in the car, feeling very much like a high school freshman catching a ride to school.

"Hey, y'all!" I said, buckling myself in between two car seats. Our children are the same age, but you would never know it because her car doesn't look like a dumpster on wheels, which is something I thought was normal, until that moment in the back seat of her car.

I looked to the left. No animal cracker crumbs. I looked to the right. No crushed, discarded juice boxes. And then I couldn't help myself. I lifted a car seat up ever so slightly…

"*Aha!*" I exclaimed, pleased as punch with my crumby discovery.

"MK, what *on earth* are you doing?" Melissa asked.

"I was checking under your car seat for crumbs."

"Umm, okay…but we will be at lunch in like five seconds."

"I just had to know if your car seat had crumbs under it!"

"First of all, you are so freaking weird. Second, *of course* my car seat has crumbs under it. Doesn't everybody's?"

Well, yes. I was hoping so. Because there is something deeply connective about the fact that we are all just a little bit messy. There is some form of solidarity and comfort when you look at somebody else's imperfect life and see a little bit of your own reflected back to you.

Do you know why Melissa is so precious to me? Because she lets me see the crumbs in her life, and she doesn't explain them away. Even though she's got it way more together on a number of fronts than I do, there is no façade of perfection with Melissa. There are areas where she's ahead of the game, and she's got crumbs under the car seats. Duality, y'all. It's a beautiful thing. There's hope for all of us in that.

I think the reason that truth telling is so dang important (besides the fact that nobody likes a liar) is this: When we share our messy, honest selves with one another, that's when we find our deepest communities. When we talk about our struggles, mess, and failures, we connect with others who have walked those same roads.

There is no depth to the relationships we forge in the Lies of Curation. There is no security in communities we form while acting

> There is something deeply connective about the fact that we are all just a little bit messy.

like we are somebody other than the beautiful disasters that God created us to be.

When life gets messy (and believe me, it will) our ability to keep pretending will be stretched. And stretched. Eventually, it will snap. The mask will have to come off, the filters will fall away, and what's left will be a hot mess human in a room full of strangers, feeling awkwardly naked and unknown.

If you want to be loved well, then you have to allow yourself to be *known* well. And the only way that can happen is if we step out boldly as truth tellers, acknowledge that we all have crumbs under our car seats, and start an honest conversation with the people we love about what it means to be human—holy hot mess and all.

But hear me out for a second, okay? Baby steps will get you started on this. I've got girlfriends who would never dream of going to the grocery store without a full face of makeup and a well-styled outfit. I don't begrudge them their immaculate grooming. Honestly, I'm amazed.

But can I tell you how honored I am when one of those friends shows up for coffee, fresh-faced with a hasty ponytail? It lets me know that I'm trusted. That I'm a person who is allowed in their mess. And maybe that's a place that anyone can start: getting bolder about the Clean Face Club. Or, maybe it's inviting some friends over for dinner and *not* making yourself crazy trying to turn your whole house into an HGTV premiere. Leave the shoes littered on the staircase. Let the Legos on the floor be. People who love you don't care about those things. Anyone else can kick rocks.

And here's a question I've been wrestling with myself: Whose standard of perfection am I trying to live up to, anyway? Nobody can clear that bar. Mess is an equal opportunity definer. We all have crumbs under our proverbial car seats. Maybe mine are all over the chair and scattered on the floormats. Maybe you have a microscopic speck of Goldfish cracker hidden beneath the buckle. Who cares? The bottom line is this, my friends: As long as we are living, there's going to be mess. We might as well get honest about it.

> **As long as we are living, there's going to be mess. We might as well get honest about it.**

Now, am I suggesting that you just pop it all open everywhere? Air out your dirtiest laundry, in front of God, the neighbors, and everybody? Um, that would be a no. Truth telling is also about wisdom. Everybody's got that gossipy cousin who loves to spill the tea. I'm *not* suggesting you share your deepest and darkest with the neighborhood Gossip Girl. What I am saying is that you should take some real vulnerability out for a spin, wisely, and see what happens. Bring store-bought cookies to the PTA meeting, when everyone else baked all morning. Don't apologize or bat an eye. Wear those flip-flops on a hot summer day; who cares if your toes look like Shrek's?

Own who you are, the skin you're in, the house you live in, the car you drive, the ragtag children you're raising.

Don't be ashamed if someone sees the crumbs in your car! It means your children are eating! Don't apologize for the toys on the stairs. It means your family has fun. Life is not Insta-worthy, my friends. If it is, you aren't doing it right. Don't shy away from imperfection and chaos. Crumbs are just *proof of life*! Authenticity is going to get messy, but that's where the good stuff is.

Authenticity is going to get messy, but that's where the good stuff is.

CHAPTER 2

URSUS ARCTOS HORRIBILIS

If the bear attacks, most experts agree that this is the moment to lie down and play dead.

> —Clint Emerson, Navy SEAL, *100 Deadly Skills:*
> *Survival Edition*

The first time I ever got stitches, I was trying to prove Momma wrong. It was the summer of the '96 Olympics, and I had gold-medal ambitions. For the non-Olympian fanatics in the room, one, get with it, and two, here's a little context: The '96 Olympics were held in Atlanta, which was just a skip and a jump away from my little hometown. That proximity of this incredible event made it feel both personal and possible. It was also the year of the Magnificent Seven, the American team of female gymnasts who were, obviously, pretty magnificent. Please tell me you remember. It was Shannon Miller, Dominique Moceanu,

Dominique Dawes, Kerri Strug, Amy Chow, Amanda Borden, and Jaycie Phelps. They won the first female gymnastics team gold for the United States in history, and the way it went down had all the makings of a weepy Lifetime movie. Tiny little Kerri Strug shredded up her ankle on her first vault for the team. The injury was agonizing, that much was clear on her face. But her team needed that vault for the gold. So, what did Kerri do? She came limping back out, vaulted again, and incredibly, she stuck the landing! Her legendary coach, Béla Károlyi, ran out to the mat and scooped her up into his big bear arms. Then, he carried her around the arena in a victory lap. If you didn't cry in that moment, yikes. You might be dead inside.

I screamed my heart out cheering for those girls. My Olympic spirit was *legit*. I leapt around the living room, wearing my bathing suit as a leotard, "training" to be part of the team. Obviously, I would be the girl who took American gymnastics to the next level. Hello, Magnificent Eight! Béla Károlyi would call (any day, now) and beg me to join the team. I was destined for Olympic glory.

Alas, those dreams were slightly complicated by the whole banned-from-the-gym-because-of-the-sock-fiasco thing. My living room lacked the necessary equipment to develop my acrobat skills. So, I convinced Momma to craft a homemade balance beam out of a few planks of lumber. With my new balance beam, I was all set…except I didn't have a coach. Eh, never mind that! I'd just watch TV! The Magnificent Seven would guide me. I'd watch Dominique's beam routine and do whatever she did. How hard could it be?

Um, hard.

Too bad enthusiasm isn't the only prerequisite for balance beam glory. If that were the case, I would have taken Atlanta by storm. In the end, an attempted toe-touch dismount resulted in a dream-killing injury. No Kerri Strug moment would be in the cards for me. I had painfully learned the meaning of the word *split*.

As a result of that experience, I decided to retire my dreams of being a gymnast, once and for all. But this wouldn't stop me from my podium moment. Oh no. My sights were still set on Atlanta. I just needed to find a new sport. One that might not come with the risk of bifurcating my body. One that would be, you know, *easier?*

I'll run the hurdles, I thought to myself. *How hard can it be to run and jump?*

I got straight back to work, making an obstacle course in the shade of our backyard. It was a hodgepodge assortment of household objects that I called my "training facility": a broom balanced atop two trash cans; a hockey stick wedged between trees. And at the end of this redneck steeplechase, a broken wrought iron gate.

I was a tigress. I was a gazelle. I was every powerful, elegant creature that has ever needed to jump over things while running. The summer sun beat down as I leapt over obstacles with athletic prowess. Momma watched on and clicked at her stopwatch.

"Good jump, MK!" she'd shout from the porch. "A little less height at the broomstick!"

With every lap, I was improving my form, efficiently clearing each hurdle. But champions aren't born—they are made by hard work! I wasn't going to be lulled into a passive pace. An Olympian pushes the envelope, y'all! I had a podium to climb.

"This time," I proclaimed, wiping sweat off my brow, "I'll hurdle with my *opposite* leg!" Switching things up, you see. How many both-legged hurdlers are out there? This would definitely give me an advantage!

"Now, wait just a minute," Momma said, setting the stopwatch down. "You're getting tired and that gate is all rusty. This seems like a bad idea."

But what did Momma know about dreams? What did she know about glory?

Children are hard-wired contrarians, y'all. Of course, I ignored her concerns.

Twenty-five stitches, a tetanus shot, and a few hours later, I was discharged from the ER. Momma was right about that stupid gate. I pushed one envelope too far. She quietly supported my elbow as I limped my way to her car. Silence was a grace I didn't deserve, but I took it all the same.

"I told you so" wouldn't be necessary. This lesson was sewn in deep. Under surgical lights, one stitch at a time, the doctor just shook his head, muttering.

"You should have listened to Momma," he said. "Momma is always right."

· · · · · · · ·

God made me a standard-issue mother. I've got no bells or whistles. Our house isn't tidy; I don't cook from scratch. My car is a dumpster on wheels. There's nothing highlighted in our family calendar, because I don't even own a calendar. I thought parenting would come naturally for me, but the truth is quite the opposite.

I'm just out in the wilderness, surviving off berries (also: caffeine, naps, and prayer).

Parenting is hard as heck, my friend. But one bit has come as easy as breathing, and that part is loving my children. There comes a moment in every parent's life when they realize just how terrifying this love can be. For me, that moment came two weeks after the birth of my son as I rocked him to sleep. He was so tiny and perfect, I couldn't stop staring at him. I inhaled the milky sweetness of the top of his head, and suddenly felt overwhelmed. It was this flood of emotions, both love and fear, and before I knew it, my mouth was moving.

"I love you so much, angel," I whispered. "If anyone ever hurts you, I'll *kill* them."

And I meant it.

At this point it seems important to note that I am not a violent person. True story: I capture flies under plastic cups and relocate them into the wild. So, I quite literally wouldn't hurt a fly. My soul belongs in an overstuffed teddy bear, but something inside me had changed. I wasn't just a momma bear; I was a momma grizzly. An *Ursus arctos horribilis*, y'all. Accent on the *horribilis*.

From the moment you become a parent, your heart moves outside of your body. There is nothing you wouldn't do, no line you wouldn't cross, to protect the child that you love. As I held my son and felt that grizzly roar within, I was

From the moment you become a parent, your heart moves outside of your body.

forced to reckon with the possibility that I had never loved anyone like this before. That before I became a parent, my life was a little bit selfish. Not that I was a jerk or anything. It was simply this: Every decision, until I had children, was made in the interest of *me*. I was out in the world, living free and wild, taking consequences as they came. But when a child is born, so is a mother. And in her, a grizzly awakens. Her love is maternal, instinctive, and deep. And when necessary, even dangerous.

> But when a child is born, so is a mother. And in her, a grizzly awakens.

• • • • • • • •

There are certain movies you watch as a kid which inspire you to do stupid things.

For me, that movie was *A Christmas Story*. If you've seen it, you know where this is going. If you haven't seen it, do yourself a favor, and go watch it now. It doesn't matter the time of the year—this movie is an evergreen classic. It's the story of Ralphie, a boy growing up in post–World War II Indiana. The film details his quest to own a Red Ryder BB gun while fighting to overcome Mom's concerns: "You'll shoot your eye out!"

Now be warned: If you're a kid watching this movie, there's a dangerous triple-dog dare that will reverberate its way off the screen and into your subconscious. It will grow to a low hum that will not go away until you do the Thing it demands of you. The *Thing* being licking a frozen pole to see if your tongue gets stuck.

One year, after watching *A Christmas Story*, I had some questions for Momma: Can I stick my tongue to a frozen pole? Would it hurt? Would the firetrucks come?

Momma didn't immediately respond. She just sighed deeply and pinched the bridge of her nose. Looking back now, I realize what my poor mother already knew: By the end of the week, there was a very strong chance that her child would be licking a pole.

I wish I could tell you I learned my lesson. That I learned to respect words of warning. But life is long, "frozen poles" are plenty…and twenty-year-olds think they know *everything*.

• • • • • • •

It was three a.m. after a long night of partying when I called my Momma, crying. I had been in college a whole four months, and my world was falling apart. First, I started drinking, and then I started dating a frat boy. The combination was a recipe for heartbreak. I knew Momma would be disappointed when she heard my slurred words, and I was embarrassed by my hiccupping sobs. But all I wanted in the whole wide world was to hear my Momma's voice. Because finally, after all those years of ignoring her warnings, after stitches and broken bones and even a tongue stuck to the freezer door (there weren't any frozen poles in southern Alabama), I had finally come to realize: My momma was always right.

Behind every pain, there was a bad choice. And behind every bad choice, there was a warning from my mother.

Don't jump that gate; you're tired.

Don't touch that stove; it's hot.

Don't date that boy; he'll hurt you.

She wasn't trying to steal my sunshine. She wasn't trying to cramp my style. She wasn't some killjoy know-it-all who couldn't let me live for myself.

She was a mother whose heart existed outside of her body. Who loved me ferociously and wanted to keep me from harm. Her hopes and plans for me were always for my good.

I wish I could have seen it then. It would've saved me so much pain. But at least, at thirty-six years old, I can see it now.

• • • • • • •

Are y'all ready for some crazy news? We are the grown-ups now. Does that ever slam into you the way it does for me? I mean, who decided it was a good idea to release us into the wild? To make decisions about adulty things like elected officials and retirement funds and bedtime, for heaven's sake? And yet here we are, you and me, with mortgages and debit cards. With car seats containing actual humans who expect us to have all the things: snacks, life wisdom, readily available Band-Aids. It's scary sometimes, but we're doing it.

Even though I'm a confessed hot mess, my two little babies trust me. Every day, despite my general not-with-it-ness, they consider me their North Star. It's wild that they think I know what I'm doing. I wonder where they got the idea. Lord knows I fail them on a regular basis, on matters both big and small.

Maybe they simply trust the fact that I'll be there whenever they need me. That a momma always has your back, no matter how messy things get. Just like I knew that my momma would be there when I called her tipsy from college, my children understand there is nothing on earth that could threaten my love for them. They are the heartbeat outside of my chest, and I'd do anything to protect them. God forbid someone test that theory and meet *Ursus arctos horribilis*.

Momma always has your back, no matter how messy things get.

• • • • • • •

Nine weeks was a standard assessment period for most of my adolescent life. That meant every two months, I got a hardcopy reminder of what a mediocre student I was. My teacher always sighed when handing over my report card. "You could do better, MK." My test scores showed above-average intelligence, but my report card showed I didn't care. And yet, every semester, there was an honor roll ceremony that I was forced to attend. First, the A and A/B students lined up on the lunchroom stage. Then, one by one, the principal called their names, shook their hands, and pinned a blue or red ribbon on their shirts. After the ceremony, a teacher's aide walked around the lunchroom, handing out stickers to everyone else that said SUPER EFFORT! The whole thing felt really freaking patronizing, even to a school-aged kid. To be fair, they did try to sweeten the deal by handing out Taco Bell coupons. The honor roll kids got a whole value meal, but the rest of us? Cinnamon twists. Who the heck drives all the way to Taco Bell for a tiny pouch of *cinnamon twists*?

Let me answer that question: my Momma.

She made the absolute most out of my absolute least. She celebrated the fact I existed. Of course, she wanted me to apply myself, to try harder as a student in school. I'm sure it kept her up at night. She is a mother, after all. But her pride in me, her motherly love, was *never* performance based. She wanted nothing more than for her daughter to be a "blue ribbon" student. But if that's not where I was, no matter the reason, she accepted me all the same. More than that, she fought for my joy. She celebrated every small win.

I remember waiting in the Taco Bell drive-thru for who knows how long with my momma. With a ginormous grin, she handed a coupon to the drive-thru attendant.

"My daughter just finished another nine weeks at Girard Elementary School!" She beamed. The woman in the window just smiled politely and handed over my cinnamon twists. The fanfare made my cheeks turn red. Her pride in me was embarrassing.

As I nibbled my cinnamon twists on the way home, I felt a growing unease. The truth is, I wanted nothing more than to bring home that stupid blue ribbon. Not because my mom was ashamed. Clearly, she was quite the opposite. It's because she loved me and believed in me, y'all. I *wanted* to make her proud. I wanted to see her face light up when I finally brought home my best.

• • • • • • •

So often we struggle in our relationship with God because we view Him through a human lens. We've had earthly relationships in which in order to receive love, we had to perform a certain way. We've had loving relationships that, out of nowhere, fell apart in our hands. So, in that same way, we spend our days expecting a shoe to drop from heaven. We assume that, in order to receive God's love, we must continue to earn it. That if we come before Him bearing cinnamon twists, He'll scoff and shoo us away. But that's not the heart of our loving Father. He makes the most of our very least. He isn't as interested in your "report card" as He is concerned for your joy.

There's a certain kind of love that, when lavished upon you, can leave you feeling uneasy. It's that humbling, unearned pride of a parent that exists when you don't deserve it. Perhaps you are familiar with that brand of love and have your own grizzly momma. Now take that ferocity and multiply it by infinity— that is how big God's love is.

Perhaps your parents failed you miserably, and you've never known a ferocious kind of love. To you, my friend, I am so very sorry. But please, take comfort in this: That enormous, unearned parental love is alive in the heart of your Father. His Heavenly love for you is perfect, unending, and deep.

And when necessary, even dangerous.

> **Parental love is alive in the heart of your Father. His Heavenly love for you is perfect, unending, and deep.**

CHAPTER 3

A TALE OF TWO T—UM, I MEAN, CITIES

It was the best of times, it was the worst of times, it was the age of wisdom, it was the age of foolishness, it was the epoch of belief, it was the epoch of incredulity, it was the season of Light, it was the season of Darkness, it was the spring of hope, it was the winter of despair.

—Charles Dickens, *A Tale of Two Cities*

The summer before I started sixth grade, I got an unfortunate case of The Boobs.

Mom said this was all due to genetics, but recently I read an article that said girls' bodies were developing early back when I was a preteen because of all the growth hormones companies put in the milk back then. I don't know whether to blame Granny

Gertie or the whole "milk does a body good" marketing gurus, but frankly, it doesn't matter much. All I know is right about the time my guy friends started talking like squeezed frogs, I started looking like Pamela Anderson's kid sister.

To further complicate matters, I was a football-playing tomboy who wasn't ready to accept this feminine fate. What a horrible sting of betrayal I felt when a perfectly thrown spiral landed against my chest that summer. A fiery shot of pain sent me to the ground, writhing around like a salted earthworm. It was my first dropped pass of the season, and the entire team was livid.

"What the heck, MK?" the quarterback shouted. "That pass was *perfect*!"

He wasn't wrong. And what was there to say? We lost the game by one touchdown, and I spent the rest of the afternoon with my face stuffed in a pillow, mourning the severe injustice of puberty.

That night was the first time that I prayed God would make my boobs fall off.

Summer came to an end, and God didn't answer that prayer. *Nope.* I just kept on growing. So being the sixth grader that I was, I came up with the brilliant solution of wearing four sports bras at a time, one on top of the other, until my chest was practically concave. I was pleased as punch with this idea and everything was working just fine.

That was, until the day Momma picked me up from school and informed me that we were going shopping. "It's time to get an appropriate bra," she said. "You look like a giant tube of sausage is sitting on your chest." I opened my mouth to protest, but she cut me off. "You can't just make curves *disappear*. When you smash them down, they have to go *somewhere*. It's science, sweetie."

"Well, I hate science," I responded.

Momma continued on, reiterating that *no child of hers* was going to walk around town looking like a Jimmy Dean smuggler. What I needed, she explained, was something called "underwire support."

"We are going to Sears."

Apparently "underwire support" was the kind of thing you could buy in the same building as washers, dryers, and linens designed by washed-up supermodels.

At Sears, we weaved our way to the back of the store, where I had to perform a TSA-level strip-down for a very old lady who smelled like baby powder but looked like a construction worker. It was a discombobulating combination. She was holding an actual measuring tape, and I'm pretty sure she was wearing a hard hat. Maybe I made the hard hat up, but that's definitely how my brain remembers it. Anyways, Grandma Baby Powder asked me to spin around, half naked, hands out, while she clucked and measured my body. Honest to goodness, I felt like a pig being inspected at the county fair.

"Are we done yet?" I squeaked, pining for the beginning of the day, when I didn't know this horror show of an experience existed.

"No," she responded, before scribbling down some numbers and shuffling away. She left the dressing room door wide-freaking-open for God and Moses and everybody. My momma pulled it shut with a look of sheepish apology, but there would be no forgiveness for this betrayal. I would rather sneak ten thousand Jimmy Deans out of the Piggly Wiggly stuffed in my shirt than be handled like a county fair ham, and she knew it. Right on cue, in walked Grandma Baby Powder with a handful of Pepto-pink undergarments.

"I am *not* going to wear those," I said.

"Young lady, you are lucky Sears has your size at all. We don't usually carry cups this large."

This large?

My eyes widened at the notion that sixth grade me was so *over the top* that even Sears couldn't help me. I mean, doesn't Sears sell *everything*? I was pretty sure I had seen a tractor back in the men's section. I started to sniffle. Mom turned to the bra salesclerk and whispered that we'd take both.

"She hasn't even tried them on—"

"We'll take them," Mom snipped.

That night was the second time I prayed for God to take my boobs away.

• • • • • • •

Fifteen years and four cup sizes later, I was a brand-new mother to six-pound, eleven-ounce Benjamin Ty Backstrom. His latch was terrible, and I couldn't breastfeed if my life depended on it. So—as if I couldn't hate my boobs any more than I already did—I was introduced to a fantabulous contraption known as a breast pump. If you are a mom, you just subconsciously covered your boob with your hand as a protective measure. *Yeah, I saw that.*

If you aren't a mom, what you need to know is this bulky,

loud machine attaches to your boobs and sucks them into strange shapes, yelling *WEE WAH WEE WAH WEE WAH* for hours on end. It milks you like a cow in the most dehumanizing way possible. Sometimes you do this from the comfort of your home. Sometimes you do this sitting on the toilet in the office bathroom while eating a granola bar and praying the phone doesn't ring because you only have a ten-minute lunch break and your boobs are about to explode.

Want to know something nobody told me before becoming a mom? Your breast pump will talk to you. Ask any mother, I promise you she heard it. I heard it. We all did. Mine said "Kardashian."

Kar-DASH-ian. Kar-DASH-ian. Kar-DASH-ian.

For hours and hours and hours.

Kar-DASH-ian.

And if you've ever heard the saying "there is no use crying over spilled milk," try pumping through a brutal case of mastitis in the bathroom at work while the breast pump murmurs *Kar-DASH-ian. Kar-DASH-ian.*

Imagine standing up after twenty minutes, only to spill six ounces of milk all over your black business skirt.

Oh, girl. You *will* cry over spilled milk. I sure as heck did.

That moment, staring at a bathroom floor covered in liquid gold, was the third and final time I would plead with God to take away my boobs.

"*God*, I can't even breastfeed *right*!!! What's the point of these things?"

That day, I decided if God wasn't gonna snap his fingers like Thanos and rid me of this burden, I was gonna pay a surgeon to do it. And after I weaned my daughter, that's exactly what I did.

The day of my breast reduction, I was so excited I could hardly sleep. What was it going to be like, having a normally pro-portioned body? Could I wear one bra at a time? Would I be able to do a cartwheel without knocking myself out? When I woke up from anesthesia, I freaked out. "I can see my belly button!" I exclaimed, as if this was a novelty unknown to humans before that moment in time. On the way home, I wore a button-up shirt for the first time since fifth grade. At long last, the buttons didn't gape over my ginormous chest. I couldn't wipe the smile off my face.

This is what answered prayers feel like, I thought.

And I rode that wave of happiness for six whole days until my follow-up appointment. Then, everything hit the fan.

Walking into the surgeon's office, I saw panic wash over the receptionist's face. We had become very friendly over the course of my visits, and she typically called me by my first name.

"Oh, Mrs. Backstrom," she said, with a bit too much formal-ity. "Isn't anybody with you?"

"Er, no," I responded. "I haven't been on any medication for four days, so I drove myself. Is that okay?"

"Of course, it is!" she said in a way that told me it was exactly the opposite of okay. "Just…just…wait right over here."

She picked up the office phone and made a few shushed calls. Something was definitely up. When I was finally called back from the waiting room, the surgeon suggested that I sit down.

Now, I am essentially a human loaf of bread. I always want to sit down. Sitting down is my favorite pastime. But something about a surgeon telling you to sit down is just a little bit unnerving. I fumbled in my purse for my phone. I had the growing suspicion that this conversation might result in a call home.

"So, how are you feeling?" my surgeon asked.

"I wish I had done this years ago! My neck hasn't hurt since I woke up from surgery. I have been wearing button-ups *every day*! It's the greatest thing ever. I am *so* happy."

"Good!" she responded with a pained smile. "I'm so glad you have recovered so quickly. MK, I'm going to jump right to this. In an abundance of diligence, my office tests the tissue samples we remove during breast reductions. We send them to an outsourced lab, where they are reviewed by pathologists for possible traces of disease. Findings are rare but can be lifesaving. Unfortunately, we identified cancer in your breast tissue."

I sat on that cold metal chair and felt the blood drain from my hands and feet. My ears were buzzing. I felt like I was watching this entire scene play out in a movie. This wasn't happening to me.

"I'm sorry. Can you repeat that?"

"After your surgery, multiple slides of tissue were tested for possible disease. You have breast cancer, Mary Katherine. My recommendation is we consult for an immediate mastectomy. I could recommend a few surgeons that I have worked with, if that would help."

I couldn't understand the words coming out of my doctor's mouth. Did she just say *mastectomy*? Doesn't that mean…cutting my boobs off? Like…*off*-off?

"I'm sorry. Did you say mastectomy? And…cancer?"

"Can we call your husband or somebody?" she offered. I

mumbled a little bit about how he had been working all night and probably just went to sleep. She responded, "I'm sure he'll understand," and quietly left the room.

"You know what's funny?" I asked the remaining nurse, holding back tears. "I've spent my entire life praying that God would take my boobs away. Seriously. My *whole life*. And now? I guess I won't have any."

The whole thing was so dark with irony that I couldn't help but laugh. But I felt my shoulders shaking, and I could tell a meltdown was coming.

Then, that nurse—a woman I had never spoken with beyond *hello* and *have a good day*—took my hand and sat right beside me.

"I'm not a doctor or a minister or anything like that," she began. "But I have been working in this office for quite some time. And I can understand how you'd be mad at God. But— *hear me out*—this was quite a miracle."

No. Nope. No thank you.

I didn't want to hear how cancer was a miracle, especially ten seconds after receiving my diagnosis. What I wanted to do was rip my hand out of hers and storm out of the room. And maybe, if I wasn't still in shock, I would have.

"You are, what? Thirty-four years old?" she asked, and I nodded my head in response.

"Well, you wouldn't have started breast health screenings for another five or ten years, at least. But you elected to have this surgery. We did a mammogram beforehand, and nothing showed up. We did a physical exam. Nothing showed up. And after your surgery, we *just so happen* to screen the tissue, and what do they find? Cancer that is early and *still treatable*. This cancer would have progressed, undetected, for years. And then, maybe it wouldn't have been treatable."

I felt my anger hollow out and the tears began to pour. The idea that some nefarious disease was lurking in my body all this time, growing, preparing to pounce, made me feel sick. But the nurse was right. All of a sudden, my diagnosis didn't feel so much like a shot to the heart.

In fact, I was starting to see it as something else entirely: a dodged bullet.

She gave my hand a final squeeze and rose from her chair.

"I can't imagine how hard this is. But just think of this: You get the chance to live out the rest of your life with those precious babies of yours. This surgery saved your life."

When she left the room, I fell to my knees and prayed.

• • • • • • •

Here's what I'm not gonna do. I'm not gonna make light of the unexpected, tragic, baffling things that have happened in your life. I don't want to turn your hurt and your questions into some cheesy Hallmark card filled with pastel puppies and platitudes. And I'm sure as heck not gonna bust out singing Garth Brooks's "Unanswered Prayers." I understand how cosmically cruel those gut-punch moments can feel.

Maybe you prayed and prayed for that guy at church to notice you, date you, and marry you. And then he did. And then ten years later he broke your heart with an affair. Or maybe you begged God for that dream job, and it turned out to be a toxic dumpster fire of harassment and headaches. Like Charlie Brown, you ran full speed at that football with blind faith. Then, at the last second, Lucy pulled it away. *Good grief.*

That's exactly what it can feel like. The ultimate *gotcha* moment.

When your prayer for your boobs to go away becomes cancer, when your prayer for that job becomes a soul-draining situation, when your prayer for the right guy becomes a broken heart, it's hard to see God in any of it. And worse, if He's there, it kinda makes you wonder: Is He intentionally breaking my heart?

To be clear, I get it. But.

God isn't pulling the football, y'all. He loves you more than that. Maybe you're in a bad spot right now, and you just rolled your eyes. I understand. I've been there, and maybe tomorrow I'll be there again. But listen to me, friend: I've lived this, too. I'm right here beside you in the trenches. When things get sideways, and God seems more invisible than ever, you can trust this truth: He is still at work. In the doctor's office, the divorce attorney's office, and in the human resources office.

He is still at work.

You and I, we have to keep looking for it. We have to continue to search for His grace in the midst of our confusion. Sometimes, it feels like impossible work. But trust me, grace always shows up. Maybe you will find it in the compassion at your attorney's office. Maybe you'll see it when you move on from that nightmare job and into a healthy work environment. Maybe God gives you the miracle of endurance in the midst of something you swore you couldn't handle. Maybe He gives you a full night of sleep after a week of all-nighters with the baby.

Sometimes, the dust settles long before you see His fingerprints, but if you keep looking, you'll see that He's there.

· · · · · · ·

Let's get back to The Boobs. I try to give credit to whom it is due, but it wasn't just a surgeon who saved my life that day. It was God, in His curiously perfect timing. For years, I had been looking forward to a reduction. But had my surgery been one single month earlier, these cells might not have been detected. Then, if I had waited a few more years, we would be discussing an entirely different prognosis. More than likely, a fight for my life.

God was bigger than all of that. He was bigger than my self-loathing and my body dysmorphia and my pain-in-the-back huge boobs. His plan, all along, was for my good.

This year, I finally got a bird's-eye glance at the intricate work God has been doing in my life. All of this time, I've felt like an ant on a tapestry, wondering where a single thread would lead. I couldn't see the big picture. And I didn't trust His plans.

The truth is, our earthly perspective is limited. We will never be able to see the whole tapestry. Not until our time on earth is done, and God's work is complete in us. Sometimes, from where we stand, it's hard to imagine how things like death and disease and pain could possibly work out in our favor.

But I'm here to tell you, *God is doing it.*

From time to time, I still laugh and tell my loved ones to be careful what they pray for. I spent fifteen years praying away my boobs, and here I am, post mastectomy, wishing I could have them back. Even if that meant visiting Grandma Baby Powder in the Sears dressing room.

The thing is, when you pray, you can count on the fact that God is going to answer. It may be in a way that you never expected. But rest assured, His ways are good. Sometimes they are confusing. Sometimes they are confounding. Sometimes they can even feel cruel.

But hold on to faith and keep your eyes on His face.

In time, you'll see it: His ways are good.

> The thing is, when you pray, you can count on the fact that God is going to answer. It may be in a way that you never expected.

CHAPTER 4

SAND AND WATER

The world breaks everyone, and afterward, some are strong at the broken places.

—Ernest Hemingway

I'm sooooo bored."

Y'all, help.

Last week, my son was bored to tears, which, to be fair, was a valid complaint. As of this writing, we're on month forever of a global pandemic, and playdates are all but extinct. So, while I empathized with my precious six-year-old, this problem wasn't exactly brand-new. I was so dang proud when he went to our art closet and pulled out some modeling clay.

"I'm gonna create a friend to play with!" he said, unpacking the clay. This seemed like a healthy (albeit tragic) response, so I pulled up a chair to encourage him.

"That's great!" I said, as he unrolled the putty and molded a humanesque figure. I cooed as he rolled out arms, a torso, and two little legs.

But somewhere between the googly eyes and *o*-shaped mouth that looked like a scream, Ben's creation took a hard left turn.

"Wow," I said, as a horror movie character was birthed on my kitchen table. "That's…that's really something, son."

Ben smiled with pride and presented to me what looked like a thumb dipped in acid.

"His name is Little Man," he declared. "And he is my new best friend."

Great.

For the next few days, that creepy creation rarely left Ben's side. Little Man wasn't large in his physical presence, only about an inch tall. But he was large in his *presence*. His creepiness filled up a room. Ben would carry Little Man around, then get distracted, and leave him propped up in random places. Leaning against the banister, beside the remote, in the cheese drawer of the refrigerator. (I have little-to-no grace for anyone or thing that desecrates the sanctity of my cheese drawer.)

And then there was the scopaesthesia. You know, scopaesthesia. Just kidding—I can't pronounce it, either, but it's the fancy-pants word for when you have that sense that someone is watching you. I'd go into a room and get that feeling of chills going up the back of my neck. I'd slowly turn, and—cue the *Psycho* soundtrack *(eee-eee-eeek!)*—there he'd be, Little Man, unblinking and unashamed, watching my every move.

Frankly, the dang thing terrified me. I'm talking to the core. Little Man was like Elf on the Shelf in dire need of an exorcism.

It belonged in a room full of porcelain dolls whose eyes move when people walk by.

One night, at bedtime, Ben casually mentioned that Little Man talked in the night. Please read that twice before you judge my next move: That freak show *talked in the night*. Or that's what Ben said, and he's usually reliable. Something had to be done.

I refused to be taken out of this world by the fingerless hands of a clay demon. I would put Ben to bed, grab some matches, and cleanse Little Man with fire. Okay, maybe not. That would be a bit much. I'd probably just throw him in the trash. Either way, my judgment would be carried out. Little Man had haunted my cheese drawer for the very last time.

A few days later, my son noticed the absence of his Acid Thumb Friend.

"Mommy, have you seen Little Man? I can't find him anywhere," Ben said. His little eyes were so pitiful, y'all. But I couldn't dare lie to his face, truth teller that I am.

"Son, I'm sorry. I thought you were done with Little Man, so I threw him away. I'll help make a new one, if you want!"

Ben looked at me as if I'd kicked a puppy. Or worse, like I'd trashed his best friend. Which, I suppose, is exactly what I did. But, c'mon. Little Man was a clay thumb with googly eyes. Who could miss such a disaster?

"No," Ben replied, his eyes filling with tears. "I don't want another friend. I know he looked funny and his eyes were falling off, but he was the only Little Man in the world."

• • • • • • •

Now, this is totally random, but I promise there's a reason I'm sharing it with you, okay? I came across the strangest study yesterday, when I most definitely should have been sleeping. But, that sliver of my day that starts when the kids fall asleep is the only time when nothing is pulling at me. Not the next thing to do, not the next place to be, not the child screaming across the house for me to wipe their butt.

Some nights, I unwind on the couch with a good book and maybe indulge in a little ice cream. Other nights, I read the April 1907 issue of *American Medicine* featuring a paper by Dr. Duncan MacDougall. You know. *Balance.*

Anyways, the paper was titled "Hypothesis concerning Soul Substance together with Experimental Evidence of the Existence of Such Substance." In plain English, this guy hoped to weigh the human soul. Which, I suppose, would empirically prove it exists, right? It was a fascinating experiment in which Dr. MacDougall placed six dying patients on a specially designed bed. He weighed them before their death, and then immediately after their passing, and the results were pretty wild. The doctor concluded that at the moment of death, there was a consistent, quantifiable weight loss. It averaged about three quarters of an ounce, or approximately twenty-one grams.

He controlled the results for considerable factors such as bowel eliminations and skin moisture loss but was unable to account for the change when the controls were in place. This is where the study got weird(er). The doctor didn't believe dogs had souls, so he gathered up about fifteen of them and did the same before-and-after experiment. How he managed to get that many dying dogs concerns me more than a little, but nevertheless, his results were conclusive: no weight loss at the moment of death. This is how he determined that humans have souls and dogs do not,[1] and that the human soul weighs twenty-one grams.

I could have saved Dr. MacDougall a whole lot of time and simply pointed him to music. I could have walked him up to the edge of the ocean and asked him to find where it ends. There is a wealth of evidence in our everyday lives that point to the soul's existence. We know it's there, stirring within us: the essence of who we are. Beyond the brain matter and deeper than the cells, there is our longing for something eternal. Dr. MacDougall felt it, and it sent him searching in deathbeds and science and dogs.

I imagine we all search in our own special ways. Perhaps that's the journey of life. There's a force within us, urging us forward, guiding every choice that we make. The people we love, the jobs we choose, the names we bestow on our children. It holds us up in our moments of grief; it feels light in our moments of joy. It's that piece of you that soars when you first hold your child. It's what bears the weight of your darkest grief. It's your resilience in struggle, your curiosity about the universe, what links you to all of humanity. It's a mystery that can't be defined by science or quantified on a deathbed scale. It's a God-like substance that calls out to its Creator. It's a bit more than twenty-one grams.

• • • • • • •

---

1   I would like to interject my scientific opinion that dogs most definitely have souls, and they probably just weigh a whole lot less because they are fun-sized and don't live very long.

I am elbow-deep in trash water, searching for Ben's Little Man. If I can find it—big, fat *if*—the thing will be smelly and ruined. Last night, raccoons opened the lid of my outdoor trash can, and between the Florida rain and heat, our garbage has turned into sludge. I'm pretty sure a one-inch-tall clay person wouldn't survive this hot trash soup. I need to take a shower and call it a day, but my heart is heavy with conviction. Children's tears are a mother's kryptonite. This is my fault. This is my mess. This is my burden to bear. I push around leftover McDonald's bags and bones from a rotisserie chicken, dry-heaving and cursing the sun. My husband gets home from work, steps out of his car, and stops to stare. He is speechless.

"I am trying to find Little Man," I puff, pushing a sweat-drenched strand of hair from my eyes. "I threw it away yesterday."

"That little clay thing?"

"Yeah."

"Oh, babe," he responds. "Oh, no."

"Look, I don't need the lecture…"

"No, it's just…I saw it in the trash yesterday, and I knew how much Ben loved it…so I figured it was a mistake. Anyways, I pulled it out and it's in the bowl on the counter."

As I stand by that trash can, smelling like a swamp monster, all I want in the whole wide world is to hug my husband violently. He politely refuses, so I run inside and wash my arms in the sink. I loudly proclaim the wonderful news that Little Man is alive and well. My son grabs his misshapen clay friend, and with a snaggletoothed smile, runs back down the hall to his room. I guess sometimes it's hard to see the beauty in something, unless you're the one that made it.

• • • • • • •

I'm going to level with you right now and admit that I am having the year from hell. January started out just fine. I scheduled a surgery I'd been waiting to have ever since my mastectomy. Finally, after two years of waiting, my body was going to be restored to a somewhat recognizable state, and then, with a fresh pair of cancer-free boobs, I would travel the country promoting my first book—2020 was shaping up to be the Year of Answered Prayers. I would be a published author! My body was on the mend! Sunshine and bluebirds and roses, y'all. You know where this is going.

And then, February came. Everyone has their own pandemic story, but mine goes a little like this: My husband is an ER physician working the front lines, and like every other doctor in the country, he needed more PPE than was available. By March, my family had contracted COVID-19, and I was critically ill. It was the scariest thing that I've ever walked through, and I hate even writing about it. Ian and I were confined to our beds, and our children had to fend for themselves. They were six and four. That's not a thing they were exactly prepared for. But, with the information we had at the time, quarantine was all but required. And that meant we were alone, no family or friends, no outside assistance with the kiddos. I have never felt so helpless. For almost ten days, we parented from our pillows, surviving on care packages left on the porch.

At the lowest point of my fight with COVID-19, I remember crying for Momma. My children were hungry and tired of Cheez-Its and smoothies. They wanted real food; they wanted a hug; they wanted their mom out of bed. But my heart rate was through the roof, my oxygen levels were in the toilet, and I needed to go to the hospital. It was the first time—not just in my adulthood, but in my entire life—that I was in crisis and my mother wasn't by my side. She simply couldn't come. She was high risk, and Florida's numbers were exploding, so her coming was out of the question. I arrived at the hospital, a party of one, scared and unsure what was next. My husband's colleagues tried to make me feel loved, but in an isolation unit, that's a hard thing to achieve. Everything, including their eyeballs, was covered. It is hard to feel some modicum of comfort when your caretakers look like astronauts.

After an initial flurry of nurses with needles and masked faces asking me questions, the room emptied out and I was left in the dark. I had nothing except an arm full of tubes and a machine that was steadily beeping. So, like many children do when they are scared and utterly alone, I called out one more time for a parent. One that I hoped might come.

Hello, God? It's me, Mary Katherine…

· · · · · · ·

I've always hated it when people remind me that God is still working on me. They always seem to mention this fact when my life is trash can soup. Like, thank you so much for that nugget of wisdom. But I'm currently swimming by chicken bones, and it's hard to see God in the sludge. What's more, sometimes I wonder if He loves me enough to care. Not that I doubt His incredible love. The thing is, I doubt that I am lovable. When

I look at my life through a critical lens, I see a whole lot of Little Man messiness. My edges aren't neat, and I don't exceed any standards: societal, biblical, otherwise. I'm an impatient parent, an imperfect spouse, an inconsistent churchgoer. I'm a crash-dieting, emotionally fragile wreck who spends as much money on therapy as tithing. I have a very hard time loving myself. All I see is a hot mess Mary Katherine who resembles an acid-dipped thumb.

But, God.

He views me through a different lens entirely. If the snaggle-toothed smile of my six-year-old son conveyed pride in his Little Man, then how much more would a holy Father find joy in a child that He made? God molded our bodies straight from clay and brought us to life with a holy purpose. His plans for us have always been good, friends. We weren't made to swim in the trash. But from time to time, we find ourselves there. That's the broken world that we live in. There is cancer, divorce, anger, and pain. There is hurt and betrayal and lies.

But that's when that part of us, that twenty-one-plus-grams, cries out that something is off. We know this isn't the way things should be. There's a standard set deep in our hearts. Our soul recognizes that our world is broken the same way we know an apple is old. There's a sweetness we long for, a taste that we've known. We were meant for better things—we can *feel* it.

So we get frustrated, and we question God's plans. Which is funny when you think about it. We were handmade with care, breathed to life by our God…and we think He'd forget about us now? He is our Father. Our tears grieve His heart. There's no trash that He wouldn't reach down in to retrieve the creation He loves. He promised us goodness, and He proved his commitment by sending His son to the cross.

Why, oh why, do we doubt?

· · · · · · ·

When my mother was in high school, she befriended a student who smoked cigarettes in the bathroom during break. Beth was a guitar-strumming free spirit whose heart came alive in music. Momma was a cheerleader, and her dad was the coach. They didn't have a whole lot in common. But the music Beth created transcended difference. She was a person living in her purpose. Their friendship was light, and it continued into adulthood, as Beth sang at my parents' wedding. She later became a hit songwriter and worked with Faith Hill, Willie Nelson, and more. Elton John performed her music. It was featured on the show *ER*. Her talent was incredible, her music impactful. But her life was never the easiest. When I was thirteen years old, Beth released an album titled *Sand and Water*. The album was a journey through the darkest side of grief, as Beth mourned the loss of her husband, Ernest. She eventually found joy on the other side, but you could hear every ragged breath of that recovery process as the album progressed. But, oh, when she made it through. In the seventh track of the album, she breaks free of grief with "Happy Girl," a song that exploded up the charts when it was later recorded by Martina McBride.

> God molded our bodies straight from clay and brought us to life with a holy purpose.

Honestly, I prefer Beth's version of that song. It was her story to tell. Her hurt and her joy, her path to the triumph of healing. Although, at thirteen years old, I'd never known a loss like hers, I felt comfort in the arc of her story. It felt as if I'd read that book before. It was as familiar to me as breathing.

Pain and overcoming. Hurt and healing. It's all part of the human experience.

In the title track, "Sand and Water," Beth wrote the following lyrics:

"Solid stone is just sand and water, baby. Sand and water, with a million years gone by."

Those are the lyrics that finally helped me stop doubting God's plan for my life. We don't have the eternal perspective that allows for a million years of patience. We don't get to look down from heaven, with an all-knowing smile, and know that the waves are essential to the outcome. We just feel the pressure, the relentless tide. And we cry out to God, in our darkest moments. "Father, what is Your plan for me?"

God is not some sort of ambulance chaser, following behind the catastrophes, hoping to clean up the mess. No. He wounds us like a surgeon, for the very purpose of our healing. We are the sand, crying out for relief, as wave after wave comes at us. God does not relish our pain. A child's tears are a parent's kryptonite, remember? But He knows the process is necessary for the outcome. He is doing a work in us, friends. You can bet that He'll see it through.

Solid stone is just sand and water, baby. Sand and water, with a million years gone by.

CHAPTER 5

GHOSTS AND GUINEA PIGS

It's a curious thought, but it's only when you see people looking ridiculous, that you realize just how much you love them.

—Agatha Christie

(Disclaimer: I must start this chapter by apologizing to my little brother, Ty. The tales I told him when we were kids were cruel and downright terrifying. Thankfully, he survived life with two big sisters and turned into an awesome, well-adjusted adult. I'm not saying that makes anything I'm about to tell you okay. But he turned out fine, so that has to count for something...right?)

I was a bored and lonely ten-year-old the summer Charlie first appeared in our family home. I use the word *appeared* rather loosely, because Charlie was a ghost. He liked to turn on the sink in our powder room and slam the occasional screen door. He would start the microwave and leave it running and once he even carved a spooky message in the trunk of our crab apple tree.

L.M.R.I.P., it said. That meant "Let me rest in peace."

Obviously.

At this point, I'm hoping you know me well enough to deduce that Charlie was a figment of my imagination. Life was sometimes isolating for a quirky latchkey kid growing up in a small town, and Charlie helped spice things up a bit.

But nobody needed to know all of that back then, least of all my nine-year-old kid brother. A few weeks into our family ghost's appearance, some neighborhood kids gathered at our house, thoroughly spooked by a recent outbreak of ominous tree carvings. It was the summer of 1995, and Charlie's antics had spread beyond my family's crab apple trees and into the yards of my playmates. Now, my playmates were kids of the '90s, and they had watched enough of the original (and far spookier) *Unsolved Mysteries* to know that hauntings could "escalate." After some serious discussion over a couple of Yoo-hoos, the gang determined that something had to be done about Charlie, and quick.

Thus, the first ever chapter of Detective Ghost Spies (DGS) was formed.

Because I had the most firsthand knowledge about Charlie (*how strange*), I was elected president, which meant I was in charge of…well, whatever it is that Detective Ghost Spies do. My first move was creating a three-ring binder with DGS written across the front in big block letters. The idea was to document every tree carving, running sink, or creak in the hallway.

If something went *hoo* in the night, we needed to write it down. Those were the rules.

The Detective Ghost Spies were amazed at my ability to find the most obscure messages carved in the tiniest letters on the most random neighborhood trees. The kids were just clever enough to determine that I had a peculiar connection to Charlie, an inexplicable ability to track his ghostly steps.

I was having the time of my life, playing the roles of both ghost and hunter. What started out as a pretty boring summer was suddenly filled with new friends and adventure.

It was all pretty tame. That is, until the morning I discovered a headless chipmunk lying prostrate across the back stoop.

It took me a minute to register what I was looking at, with the missing head and whatnot. I was equal parts horrified and fascinated by the thing, and I couldn't help but lean down closer to get a better look. I figured a neighborhood cat had left it as some kind of twisted love offering.

Bleh.

"Hey, sis!" my brother yelled from his perch in a magnolia tree. "Whatcha looking at?"

"Hey!" I hollered back, motioning with my arm. "Get over here!"

As Ty climbed down from the tree, I sighed. It just occurred to me that Momma was not going to be happy about two-thirds of a chipmunk being splayed out on her doormat. We would need to bury it before she got home, and I would *much* rather be playing with my DGS friends than…*gasp!*

That's when it hit me, an idea so brilliantly twisted that I'm still creeped out to this day that my little-kid brain came up with it. As my brother trotted up beside me, his green eyes widened at the spectacle before him.

"Go and grab the DGS binder, Ty," I whispered. "Charlie has done something *horrible*."

That night, an emergency DGS meeting was held, and I announced to the team that we had a real problem on our hands. You see, it seemed our little specter, Charlie, had initiated a bona fide Chain of Death.

"Chain of Death?!" the kids gasped as we huddled under a blanket fort with our flashlights. Lucky for them, I was just the right person to explain such a thing.

"A COD is the final phase of a haunting," I said. "Right before a ghost goes back to the other side, he lashes out at the world. The good news is, Charlie won't be around much longer. The bad news? That chipmunk was probably just the beginning."

Over the next few weeks, I was proven right. The Chain of Death racked up a plethora of backyard victims. Bunnies, squirrels, and robins came trickling in, mangled, headless, and lovingly placed on our back stoop.

After a while, some questions began to arise within the DGS ranks.

Was it possible Charlie could come after a kid? If so, who would it be? Were our pets safe? Should we tell an adult?

I was beginning to regret the fact that Charlie's shenanigans were now inexorably hitched to some stupid, feral cat. I had unwittingly lost control of the entire situation. Playing ghost was invigorating at first, but now the kids were losing sleep and freaking out, and honestly, this had snowballed pretty far beyond slamming a few screen doors.

Lucky for me, a miraculous reprieve came in the form of an elderly lady who moved into the little blue cottage across the street. She was a waif of a woman who set milk bowls out every morning and tuna bowls out every night, drawing in every feral cat within a ten-mile radius. This was much to the chagrin of the neighboring adults, who would call one another on the weekend, spinning phone cords around their fingers and yammering on about rabies and animal control and angry mating noises.

But I didn't mind Miss Lonnie. Because when she arrived, just like *that*, the Chain of Death was finally over. For the next few weeks, not a single headless critter was to be found. And to the members of DGS, that meant our mission was finally complete.

Early one Saturday evening, the Detective Ghost Spies ceremoniously gathered one last time. We snacked on popcorn and wrote our "testimonies" in the official DGS binder. We toasted our courage with bottles of Yoo-hoo and pondered what the other side was like. And then, with a final click of our flashlights under another blanket fort, the group disbanded.

With the mission completed, I started to worry: Would the crew come around anymore? I'd created a masterpiece mission that resulted in a summer full of magic. The clues, the ghouls, the thrill of the chase—brilliantly mapped out for adventure. I admit, the whole headless chipmunk narrative got a little out ahead of me. But Miss Lonnie and her daily dishes of milk proved to be clutch in the end. The pressure was off, as far as mission planning. And for that, I suppose I was grateful. But loneliness is its own kind of force, and I could feel it start to press in.

A few days later, once again bored and alone, I found myself plinking away at the untuned piano that sat against our living room wall. With Charlie gone, I needed to find a new hobby. So, I fiddled around for a few hours with a music book, then hung flyers all over the house announcing a recital. Everyone was invited to attend, but fancy clothes were required. Momma arrived first, wearing a black dress and pearls. My sister had gymnastics, so she couldn't attend, which left us waiting on Ty. He had accepted the invitation but was running a little late.

I was halfway through my warmup of "Hot Cross Buns" when I heard my brother enter the room, sniffling. I turned around on the bench, and there he was. Big green eyes, red cheeks, tears streaming down his face.

"Mom? I...I went to get Spike for the concert, but he fell asleep...and he won't wake up."

Momma shot me a sideways glance. Spike was Ty's beloved guinea pig, named thus for the mohawk that ran down the center of his body. Ty went everywhere with that dang rodent, and Spike even squealed when Ty got home from school.

"Well," Momma said, standing up from the couch. "Let's go see what's going on with Spike."

The three of us walked down the hallway and into my brother's bedroom and peered into the cage that held a fluffy, calico body.

What was going on with Spike wasn't a whole lot. It's what *wasn't* going on that proved to be a problem. As in moving, breathing, being alive.

Spike was dead as a doornail.

Ty started sobbing, cradling his guinea pig close. Momma headed to her closet in search of a shoebox that would serve as a casket. I gave my brother a tight hug and then followed her out of the room. All of a sudden, I had an uneasy feeling. Like maybe I shouldn't have fooled around about ghosts all summer long.

What if a Chain of Death thing wasn't something to be trifled with? What if talking about ghosts all summer long actually brought one into our house? What if I was the one who brought this tragedy down upon our house?

"Momma," I said, standing in the doorway of her closet, "I know this is...weird. But we *have* to find out what happened to Spike."

"Oh, honey," she replied, voice muffled in the depths of her closet, reaching for an empty shoebox. "I'm sure he had a heart attack or a disease or something. Who knows?"

"Is that something an autopsy could determine?"

"An...autopsy?"

"You know, when they cut the animals open and—"

"A *guinea pig* autopsy."

"Yes, because something bad could have happened and—"

"Honey. Listen. I'm sorry about Spike. We all loved him very much. But I will not call Dr. Clark and ask him to perform an autopsy on a guinea pig."

I ran to my bedroom in tears and slammed the door for dramatic effect. Flinging myself across my bed, I pushed my face into a pillow and screamed, loud and long. I can only imagine what my mother felt in that moment, standing across the house in the middle of her closet. Listening to my screams. Holding a guinea pig casket, wearing her grandmother's pearls. Wondering what in the cornbread hell just happened.

I woke up the next morning after a night of fitful dreams, full of visions of ghosts and headless chipmunks, disembodied guinea pigs and friends riding away on their bikes. The light in my room showed it to be midmorning. Momma was sitting at the foot of the bed, patting my leg.

"Hey, Muffin," she said. "How are you feeling?"

"Better," I replied, although I wasn't sure that was the case. "Did you and Ty bury Spike?"

"No, we didn't get a chance. Ty fell asleep, too."

"Oh," I said. "That stinks. Did you have to bury Spike by yourself?"

"Not exactly," she responded, with an unsure smile. "I put him in the outside freezer."

I looked at my momma. She looked at me. I suddenly didn't have any words. I didn't know whether to laugh or cry, but I was certainly too stunned to fully commit either way.

"MK," Momma soothed me. "I called Dr. Clark this morning. We talked for a good while about guinea pigs. It turns out, Spike died because he didn't have a companion."

"What do you mean? Ty did a great job with Spike!"

"No, no." She shook her head. "Spike needed a *guinea pig* companion."

Momma went on to explain that guinea pigs are social creatures that require constant company to be happy and fulfilled. Absent that deep sense of security, they can grow depressed and unhealthy, and die.

"And that's what happened to Spike?" My voice cracked at this notion.

Momma frowned and stood up from the bed.

"Why don't you get dressed, baby? I'm making French toast."

When Momma left the room, I sank deep into my pillow, pushing my fists into the corners of my eyes. I tried to will the tears to go back into my brain or wherever the heck it was that tears came from. I should have felt relief, right? After all, I hadn't accidentally conjured an evil spirit from The Other Side to slay my brother's guinea pig and kick off a whole new Chain of Death.

But no, I didn't feel relief. I felt heartbroken.

The idea that God created animals who could actually die from loneliness left a pit in my stomach and coughing little sobs inside my chest. It was oddly relatable to a weird little me who would do anything, *anything*, to gain the attention and company of some neighborhood kids—even create a ghost. I think I felt a strange and sad kinship to pitiful Spike. How a creature could look so happy on the outside while suffering inside from a deep and withering loneliness.

I lay down for a good long while, staring at the ceiling and pondering the odd connection between the souls of guinea pigs and human beings.

Eventually something drove me from that heartache, out of bed, and into the kitchen to start my day. It could have been the smell of bacon. I don't remember exactly.

But there are some things that I do clearly remember from the remainder of that day. I remember eating a plate full of

French toast. I remember getting on my bike and knocking on the doors of some fellow Detective Ghost Spies. I was holding hope that they would come over, even if our ghost Charlie wasn't going to be around. Would I be enough? Would little ole MK be enough of a draw for their companionship, or would I be a future victim of the invisible Lonely Guinea Pig Syndrome?

I remember how my heart swelled in my chest when they all jumped on their bikes and came. There was no promise of ghost hunting on my part. There was no need to consult the DGS binder. My little brother was hurting, we needed our friends around, and that was enough.

Late that afternoon, the kids pulled dining room chairs out of the house and lined them around the crab apple tree. My brother played "Kiss from a Rose" on a silver tape player as Momma walked out of the house with a shoebox holding a frozen guinea pig. The Detective Ghost Spies respectfully stood from their chairs as we lowered Spike into the ground beside our crab apple tree.

And in that moment, I couldn't help but laugh.

LET ME REST IN PEACE was conveniently carved above his grave.

• • • • • • •

I thought I'd retired from hunting ghosts, and I guess I did for a while. But it became clear to me as a grown-up that many of us are haunted. I've done some real digging to solve this mystery. So grab a Yoo-hoo and meet me at the blanket fort. This meeting is in session, friends. We have some notes to discuss.

The thing is, something is driving us to act unnaturally and conjure up stories for attention. Not about headless chipmunks, thank God. But stories, all the same. We pretend we have our crap together; we share pictures of perfectly groomed children. We get on Facebook to gush about our spouses—*My personal Prince Charming!*—as we are literally sleeping in the guest bedroom because we can't stand the smell of their farts. It's like we're possessed by this strange idea that we all need to look perfect.

The ghost of loneliness is making us crazy. We are out carving messages in trees. Except this time the message is "Please love me" and the tree is social media. I think the only thing that we want is to feel understood and seen. But the irony of all this specter building is that it's making us lonelier than ever. You will make yourself crazy keeping up this charade. Take it from me: It's exhausting playing two parts. You *have* to make a decision. You can:

1. Be yourself and put yourself out there. The truth is, you'll risk some rejection. Or…
2. You can play the role of this phantom perfect person, every day rejecting yourself.

Have you ever watched *Scooby-Doo*? As a lifelong ghost enthusiast, I love it. I don't even need my kids to be home for that cartoon to pull me in. The funny thing, which I didn't realize as a kid, is every episode is the same.

The four teenage members of Mystery, Inc. arrive in whatever city and immediately encounter a paranormal spook—which of course has its own local legend. They get to work solving the mystery while the ghost terrorizes the townsfolk. In the end, they capture and reveal the "ghost," which is always just some local crook. As the unmasked legend is taken to jail, they utter some version of these words: "And I would've gotten away with it, too—if it weren't for you meddling kids!"

This line never fails to give me a giggle. These crooks have the most ridiculous plans. "I'll just wear this fur suit filled up with balloons and fly around town like a bear!" "I'll just ski on stilts wearing this snow monster suit and scare away all the snowboarding competition!"

Really? You thought you were getting away with this ruse? My two-year-old figured you out!

It's the pattern that teaches us what to expect. It consistently points to what's real. My kids don't get scared watching these ghost stories. They know that *Scooby-Doo* villains are people, because that's the grand reveal every time. And after being alive for thirty-six years, I feel the same way about "perfect people." I would sooner believe a snow monster on stilts than a person who has no mess. I think at the heart of it, we all know better, and we want to let go of the ruse. We want to stop pretending, we want to be real with each other. So what's holding us back?

It's fear, y'all. Plain and simple. The scariest story you've ever heard is the one you are telling yourself: that if you are honest with people and share your flaws, they'll realize you are unlovable. Insecurity is haunting you and terrifying your town, but you don't have to believe it. It's just another one of Satan's lies, masquerading as truth. A Scooby Dooby–dupe (oh yes I did).

GHOSTS AND GUINEA PIGS

I'm pulling the mask off the monster for you, okay? Here's the big reveal:

You are *enough*, exactly as you are. You don't have to pretend anymore. You are more than lovable—you are already loved. By a God who made you by hand.

> You are more than lovable—you are already loved. By a God who made you by hand.

CHAPTER 6

WELCOME TO CHURCH, EVERYONE'S WEIRD HERE

Come, all you who are thirsty,
come to the waters;
and you who have no money,
come, buy and eat!
Come, buy wine and milk
without money and without cost.

—Isaiah 55:1

There is something you need to know about me: I am basically Buddy the Elf.

Hugs are my favorite. Revolving doors are my favorite. Christmas? My absolute *favorite*. Still, I somehow married a Halloween person, which I didn't even know was a thing. I mean, come on, let's compare. Pumpkins, scarecrows, and crying children? Or baby Jesus, presents, and flying reindeer?

(Be careful how you answer, Ian Backstrom. Santa Claus is watching.)

Anyways, on a Sunday morning in December, I was getting the kids ready for church. I was beyond giddy, because at three and five years old, Christmas was becoming real to them. They knew about baby Jesus and how He was born in a manger, and they knew to be on their best behavior (otherwise, they get stockings of coal). My kids were gonna shine at church this particular week, amen, hallelujah! As I walked my little cherubs through those double doors, all dressed in their red and green, I couldn't even hide my excitement. The hallway leading up to their Sunday school was decorated from top to bottom. Animals, wise men, and even the star. They'd be studying the birth of Jesus.

Ben and Holland were more than prepared for this class; we read this story year-round. They'd be making their momma proud this morning.

"Have a good morning, babies!" I sang, then shooed them into the room.

I skipped down the hall to the parenting class, where pastries were being served. I grabbed a donut and a cup of coffee and sat down at a round table.

"Hey, everyone!" I chirped with a smile. "What are we discussing today?"

"Shame in parenting," a friend replied. "Like when your kids make you feel embarrassed."

Should be a breezy discussion, I figured. Because obviously, my children would *never*.

One hour later, I was back at children's church to retrieve my precious angels. I waited at the door for the Sunday school teacher to hand me the sign-out sheet, but when Mrs. Patti arrived, she looked around all sketchy, like she had a big secret to share.

"Um, MK," she whispered, pulling me aside. "We had a thing happen today."

"A thing?" I raised an eyebrow. "What do you mean?"

"Well, we were discussing the birth of baby Jesus, and Mrs. Sara asked the children a question. She asked if anyone knew how Jesus was born, and Holland stood right up and answered."

"Okay...and what did she say?"

"She said"—Mrs. Patti leaned in closer—"'Out of Mary's *vagina*.'"

• • • • • • •

Confession time.

For most of my adult life, I've felt out of place in the church. And I am not talking about one congregation; I mean the whole kit and caboodle. I've joined churches, left churches, shopped around for new ones. I've been in leadership, deeply plugged in. I've been a drive-by member, attending on holidays. I have struggled to fit in the body of Christ, which is weird, because I *really* love Jesus. Not in that teenage, wishy-washy, puppy love way. It's way more serious than that.

Like, have you ever been at a dinner party with a friend

who is practically snoring? Then, someone mentions *Hamilton* the musical and—*boom*—they are wide freaking awake? It's like somebody lit a match under their butt. They are waving their arms as they share their thoughts. They are downright Pentecostal.

Or, think about your vegan friends, okay? You *definitely* know who they are. And that's because any opportunity a vegan has, they will tell you about their lifestyle. Because they are proud of it. Because it makes them happy. Right?

Good, we are on the same page. When I became a believer in Christ, I felt that same match under my butt. I wanted to tell the whole wide world, so that's what I tried to do. I immediately left college and bought a plane ticket to Thailand, where I volunteered as a middle school English teacher. I spent twelve hours a day on those school grounds, and on the weekends, I hosted free camps. I loved those kids because Jesus loved those kids, and it was as simple as that for me. As my students got to know me, they asked me about Jesus, and y'all, I couldn't contain myself. I came to life with my hands waving around as I told the story of my faith. About a miracle baby who was born in a barn full of stinking animals. About prophecies fulfilled and promises made and the cross that set me free.

When I tell you I love the person of Christ, this is what I mean. If a *Hamilton* fan and a vegan had a baby, that baby would be me, loving Jesus.

I love the way He threw shade at the Pharisees while deconstructing their theology of self-righteousness. I love the way He defended the marginalized and embraced children and women. Biblical culture would see an adulteress stoned to death, but nope. Not my Jesus. He looked at the people holding the stones and asked, "Who among you is without sin?"

Like, go ahead, baby. Chuck that rock! But you better watch out for the ricochet.

Jesus was radical. He was holiness and grace. I adore Him with zero chill.

So why would I feel so weird in His church—the body of Christ? My family?

• • • • • • •

It's 2009, and I am wearing a black dress and standing in front of the bathroom mirror. I am patting a cold towel against my eyes, trying to freshen my face. It's a beautiful day for a family funeral, and that counts for something, I guess. I pack some Kleenex into my makeup bag and toss it into my purse. Then I hop in the car and drive to church, where a crowd is slowly arriving.

My Poppa was a POW in World War II and kept a shoebox of relics in his closet. As a kid I would sit on his closet floor, wide-eyed with fascination, as he shared the dark history behind each item: A knife he took from an enemy soldier. A cigarette lighter that looked like a pistol. Coins from around the globe. Those are my favorite memories of Poppa. He came to life telling war stories.

As my family arrived at the church reception, the cousins clustered together by age. We hugged one another and caught up on life, sipping sweet tea from Styrofoam cups.

"Y'all aren't gonna believe this," a younger cousin whispered. "But Grandma wants a family photo after the graveside service."

"I'm sorry, what?" I replied, praying I misunderstood her.

"Yep," she said, with a grimace. "She wants all the cousins to take a picture, and then she's putting it on a Christmas card."

The cousins looked at one another in horror, then burst into a fit of giggles. A nearby relative we didn't know shushed us for laughing out loud. We huddled close together like penguins to continue our conversation.

"So what you're telling me is, after we bury Poppa, and we've all been crying for an hour in the sun…we are going to pose together, everyone wearing black, and take a picture that will be mailed to the masses?"

"Yep, you've got it," my cousin giggled. "Welcome to the Adams family."

The pun on grandmother's maiden name wasn't lost on me, and I nearly spit out my tea.

"What the heck will the card even say?" I asked. "Merry and bright?"

"Or worse," Lindsay whispered, leaning in. "The most wonderful time of the year."

We all laughed together, prompting another "Shhh!" from a nearby deacon.

"We should go," I whispered, and the others agreed. "Y'all wanna pile into my car?"

Thirty minutes later, we were under a tent at the graveside of our beloved Poppa. Hymns were sung, prayers were prayed, and we lowered his body to rest. Then, a military ensemble showed up in full regalia to present our great-grandmother, Granny, with a folded flag. It was a poignant moment, serious and heavy. There wasn't a dry eye in the crowd.

The officer knelt down in front of Granny and whispered a word of gratitude. Then he added, "Ma'am, if you wish, we can take the flag with us and return it to you in a case." At which point a relative seated nearby spoke up in a loud, country accent.

"Oh, thank ya, sir, but that won't be necessary. We're gonna shake it out later and fly it at the lake."

Now, pause. It feels important to fully unpack the significance of this faux pas.

The presentation of a folded flag is intended to be an end-of-life honor, reserved for veterans who served in times of war or made other significant sacrifices. It is typically encased in a dark wood shadow box and displayed on a wall or a mantel. Or, you know, some other place of dignity. Where it shouldn't be found is flapping in the wind at the dock, as neighbors blast Willie Nelson from their boat speakers while chugging cans of Natty Light.

The officer was wide-eyed horrified; the very idea rendered him speechless. The cousins were shaking in their seats, trying their best to hold in laughter. Momma's mouth dropped open in shock, and she intervened as best she could.

"Sir, thank you for coming, and for bringing this flag. We would like it returned in a case."

The officer nodded politely, then turned on his heels and retreated as quick as a rabbit. My family had managed to freak out a soldier. A decorated one, at that. I was relieved he wouldn't be around for our gothic holiday photo shoot.

The cousins convened later that evening for a post-funeral round of cocktails. We talked about the shoebox and we toasted Poppa's memory. We cried and we consoled one another. Then we laughed and we cringed at our family circus, and the absurdities the funeral brought forth. At the end of the evening, we hugged one another tightly, heartbroken to separate once more. Family is weird as heck, sometimes. But they are no less precious or necessary.

· · · · · · ·

After my daughter told her Sunday school class about the Virgin Mary's vagina, I walked out to my minivan in tears. I might would have gotten away with it, too, had it not been a holiday time parking lot. My distress was spotted by a couple from Sunday school, and they diverted their path toward mine.

"MK?" my girlfriend Rosie asked, concern plain on her face. "Are you okay?"

I clicked the Door Open button and shooed my children in, instructing them to buckle themselves.

"I'm fine, I'm fine," I responded lightly, hoping to discourage further conversation.

"Yeah, no. You don't look fine. Is there anything I can do?"

I paused for a second, not entirely sure how I wanted to respond. Then I remembered how vulnerable Rosie had been when we were talking about parenting shame. She put it all out there, her worst possible moments. She'd made me feel less alone.

"You know what? I could use some prayer. I'm a little bit frustrated right now."

I told her how I had worked so very hard to teach my daughter the names of her body parts. Why it mattered to me, as a survivor of sexual abuse, that she *never* feel shame using those words. I shared how much I freaking loved Christmas, and how excited I had been this morning, then how deflated I was when my daughter left class, feeling embarrassed for sharing her answer.

Rosie shook her head, and I could tell she understood.

"MK," she said, "I'm sorry. Sometimes church is like that. We don't mean to hurt or embarrass each other, but we are human. Things like that happen. I think you should talk to her Sunday school teacher. It could be a teachable moment."

I scrunched up my nose at the very idea. I was not about to go inside and monologue at a Sunday school teacher about my daughter's use of *vagina*. Hard pass. That sounds worse than the principal's office.

"Ugh, I don't think so. That would be super awkward. And anyways, it's not exactly why I came this morning."

"Oh?" said Rosie, sounding confused. "What do you mean by that?"

"It's just…I came for Christmas magic and donuts. For community and encouragement and truth."

"Of course, you did," Rosie said, with a nod. "And that's why Mrs. Patti came, too."

• • • • • • •

For years, I would leave church every Sunday both inspired and incredibly frustrated. Inspired because people make the church beautiful. Frustrated because they also make it messy. These feelings were further complicated by the fact I'd show up thinking the body of Christ should be easy. Like I could walk through the doors, get some Jesus and cranberry juice, and leave feeling fed and encouraged.

You would think, given how much I love Jesus, I would have known better than that. The *entire* reason I am drawn to Christ is that He offers abundant grace. Wouldn't it make sense that the people in church would be those who need grace in abundance?

Imagine with me for just a moment a sign at the edge of the road. It is lit up at night with flashing lights. It's bold and easy to read. It points to the entrance of the church and it says: Free bread! Free wine! Free milk! Free water!

Who do you think would show up?

The hungry, the thirsty, the poor, the needy. They would show up disheveled and tired from their journey. They would stink from their days in the streets. Maybe they'd be addicts, who've tried medicating their hurt. Maybe their teeth would be missing. They'd be a scraggly bunch, a motley crew, the people who need it most. People like you and me.

Jesus invited all to His table, but it's the hungry who show up to find Him. No wonder the church is a perpetual mess. That's exactly what God intended.

I've been a Christian for fifteen years now. I've been a member of church my whole life. But when it comes to theology and the mysteries of God, I still have more questions than answers. And yet, there are three things that I am confident of.

Three things you can take to the bank:

1. God loves all people.
2. People are messy.
3. Messy people make up His church.

It's funny to consider how maddening family can be, but how devastating it feels to lose them. I can tell you right now, as a follower of Christ, I feel the same way about church. There are days when I'm proud, days when I'm livid, days when I'm inspired to tears. Days when I swear that I'll never go back. Days when I never want to leave. But the church is no more than a group of believers, your brothers and sisters in Christ. It's going to get hard, and it's going to get weird. But trust me: It's precious and necessary.

I'm not downplaying this struggle. Heck, I had to start and restart this chapter because I would get a few hundred words in and then realize that I was ranting about church, rather than celebrating and accepting its messiness. You feel it too, right? You've volunteered for all the things. You've had leaders disappoint you. You've fallen in love with a church, and then you've seen the underbelly of how things are run. It makes *you* want to run. I understand.

So why do we even mess with it?

It's this. Church is not a building. It's so much more than that. It's a collection of people who cycle through mess like a washing machine full of laundry. If the draw of grace is that we come away clean, then it isn't for fluffy, fresh towels. Jesus came for the sweaty gym clothes and the stinky, crunchy underwear. There's more than a quick cleaning cycle required for this community. Sin has left skid marks on us all.

But something wild happens when you consistently hang out with a motley crew of believers. Community has this bizarrely cleansing effect. It helps us move past our selfishness. It stretches our ability to love. Church leaves no room for the fantasy that people of faith have it all together. These hot mess saints stand together as proof that church is not malfunctioning. It's working exactly the way it's supposed to—as a healing place for the broken.

I made my way back to church. After Christmas. After my kid was the one who said *vagina*. After Mrs. Patti's scolding. Just an average Sunday, for an average service. I sat myself on a pew among average people. The music was cheesy, the coffee was meh. But honestly, it was fine. I didn't come for a caffè Americano. I came for a cup of grace.

Church isn't about the spectacular music or the members who've got it together. It's about the pilgrims who keep showing up, straight off the waterworn boat. Disheveled and motion sick from the chaos of life. Some of them can be a little judgy, I admit. Some of them a little bit needy (raises hand). But all of us show up as less than we should be...and *that* is the purpose of church.

Maybe you're there every week. Maybe it's been years. Maybe you're in the middle of a deep love affair with your church, and maybe you've never been more disillusioned. Wherever you are, I've been there, too. But I always find my way back. Because it's so very good for us to sit among our people. To do life with our strange, messy siblings. My friend, don't give up on church because it is weird. Remember, family is weird. But it's no less precious or necessary.

CHAPTER 7

ON SHARKS AND THERAPISTS

Generally, by the time you are Real, most of your hair
has been loved off, and your eyes drop out and you get
loose in the joints and very shabby. But these things
don't matter at all, because once you are Real you can't
be ugly, except to people who don't understand.

—The Skin Horse (in *The Velveteen Rabbit*)

I was raised in the great state of Alabama, which on the sliding
scale of Places with Scary Critters falls somewhere in between
Kansas, home of prairie dogs, and Australia, home of great white
sharks and snakes that can paralyze you with their spit. I'm pretty
sure the only adorable creatures to come out of Australia are the
Hemsworth brothers. But I digress.

Growing up in Alabama, the two things I worried about most
were rattlesnakes and sharks. Hiking in the woods, folks would

always tell you, "Don't go worrying about snakes. They're just as scared of you as you are of them." But snakes have rattlebutts and venomous fangs, whereas I am a human loaf of bread with omnivorous molars. Again…who should be scared of whom?!

I wasn't buying it.

Then, when I was in high school, my dad tried to convince the family that swimming in the water on the Gulf Coast together would be great fun. Well, I had seen those shows during Shark Week, *thank you very much*, and there was no way I was getting in that water.

Y'all. Can you believe he tried to sell me that same "just as scared of you" bundle of goods—but with sharks? Yes, sharks. Who are basically underwater snakes, but with hundreds of teeth and their own horrible theme song.

No thanks, Dad. I'll stay right here.

I set up a comfy umbrella, cracked open a book, and watched my siblings splash around for hours looking like a bunch of baitfish at the shark buffet. My family was having the time of their lives, minus me. Waves were caught, memories were made, and nobody was eaten by a shark. That was nice. Sometimes the math works out that way.

Nevertheless, I did not regret keeping my fanny parked safely on the shore. The reality is, some of us are magnets for disaster. And as one of those super-special disaster magnets, I felt no need to offer my body to the ocean as an open challenge. I mean, if it's my time to go, it's my time. But I prefer not to go in a megalodon's mouth.

(God, are you listening? This one's important. Amen.)

Twenty years after my family didn't get eaten by sharks, I

grew to understand that, while phobias are still a thing, there are much scarier beings in the World of Adulthood. Remember how as kids we were convinced that quicksand was gonna be a problem?

Well, then you grow up and learn that while quicksand isn't much of an issue, there are other things that can figuratively pull a person under.

Taxes, for instance. Pretty sure most folks would rather tangle with a snake than the IRS. I mean, who keeps a receipt for an Uber they took six months ago?

And let's talk about the dentist. That office is just a bunch of open-mouthed humans making gargley stress noises while drills scream loudly in the background. That is some seventh circle horror. I'll take the quicksand, any day.

But to me, the scariest thing in the whole entire World of Adulthood is a therapist. This is because, as gentle and whispery as they are, therapists have an affinity for Jedi mind tricks. You take a seat in their office, feeling pretty good about life, and next thing you know you're sobbing about that boy in sixth grade who called you a rottweiler because you were the only girl who wasn't shaving yet.

Therapists seem so harmless before peeling your brain like an onion, leaving you feeling naked and exposed. You sit in that chair just to laugh and cry and word-vomit all of the things, and then forty-five minutes later you're forking over a hundred dollars and saying "Thank you, sir!" But of course, you set up another appointment because you *do* feel much better, even if you don't have a clue why.

Like, *what just happened*?

I was explaining this bizarre phenomenon to my husband, who for some peculiar reason doesn't go to therapy. And as I unpacked the details of how complete strangers can have the access code to your deepest pain and secrets, it occurred to me that maybe my dad was half-right all those years ago.

"Babe," I gasped, with wonder. "What if my therapist is just as scared of me as I am of him?"

"What?" Ian busted out laughing. "Honey, that's absurd. Why would a therapist be scared of you?"

"I mean…I guess I've said some weird things. You're supposed to be unfiltered in therapy, you know? Sometimes stuff just comes out."

Ian suddenly looked concerned. "Stuff like…?"

"Okay. Well, this one time Dr. C was talking, and I kinda tuned out for a second. I realized his family pictures were behind him, and it got me wondering…"

"Oh, no. MK…"

"It got me wondering if it was wise for him to have his family pictures on his desk because, you know, he deals with crazy people all the time!"

"You didn't say that."

"Well, of course I did. He asked me what I was thinking about! So, I told him he must not deal with many dangerous people since he kept his family pictures all over his office. And honestly, I think he was a little scared."

"You don't say!"

"I wasn't making a threat!"

"Wow," he said. "That is actually horrifying."

"I'm just *unfiltered*, you know? Like, Tuesday I zoned out again, and he asked me what I was thinking about. Well, I was thinking about how, when I was a child, I tried to see if the iron was hot by spitting on it. So I did, and it sizzled and then smelled bad. And that made me wonder if evaporated spit was basically how my breath smelled and it gave me a complex about breathing for like two years."

Ian was rubbing his forehead.

"Babe, he's obviously not scared. He scheduled me for even more appointments."

"I'm sure he did, MK," Ian laughed. "Do me a favor, okay? At your next appointment, I need you to let me know if Dr. C still has his family pictures up."

The following Tuesday, I sat across from my therapist and looked around the room. He smiled and asked me, in a whispery cadence, how I was doing. His family pictures were nowhere to be seen.

I was thirty-six years old when I realized that *people are just as scared of us as we are of them*. Even therapists—and they are people experts!

So what do we do with that information? How do we respond to the idea that sometimes the very core of who we are is enough to make others feel threatened or uncomfortable?

It's tempting for us to shrink within ourselves. I mean, the idea of being Boldly You is all well and good, until you crack a joke in a crowded room and the only response you get is chirping crickets. It's in those moments that we can be tempted to believe that we are just "too much" for some people.

And so we shrink ourselves down.

We keep the quirky joke in our mouth. We filter our vulnerable thoughts. We zip ourselves into a neat, unoriginal suit and wear it around the world, hoping people will love us a little bit more if we aren't so strange and scary.

That's option one. And hey, I understand. Sometimes standing out means standing alone. And standing alone can be pretty dang terrifying.

But what about option two?

Listen. I am the poster child of awkward authenticity, and at times it has left me sitting in front of a crowd, feeling utterly freakish and alone. It's true that I found myself back in front of my therapist, who stared at me like I might be a rattlesnake in his chair.

But over the course of my life, I have grown to accept these moments as a necessary tension. I have lived entire seasons of my life trying things the other way, and I remember how hollow that felt. Do you remember high school? How you smoothed out your rough edges and edited your crazy ideas and hoped that would win you a place at the lunchroom table?

Lord, I remember.

Over the course of four years I figured out that with a little less salt and a little less spice, I could tone myself down enough to be accepted by my peers. With practice, I finally earned a place at their proverbial lunchroom table.

And it felt like existing in a sleeve of crackers. There was no richness in that life.

• • • • • • •

Here's what I've figured out about this shrinking phenomenon: It's an instinctual response to fear. It's what happens when we think we might be rejected or hurt. God gave the turtle the ability to pull all of its parts in and hide, and we have a similar response. We retreat into our shell, make ourselves smaller. People can't hurt what they don't see, right?

But does this kind of shrinking make God happy? Is this how He wants us to live? I decided to seek the answer the way any modern theologian would. I googled it. *Does the Bible say anything about shrinking?* I typed. My assumption was no. I couldn't imagine a biblical context in which the word would make any sense.

But when I hit that Return button, I was shocked to see a whole bevy of stuff come back in the search.

Like...there was this one verse that talked about a woman whose thigh was shrinking, and I was all on board for that one. Some holy thigh shrinkage sounds amazing. But, upon further inspection, it wasn't some Bible time miracle diet; it was a test of infidelity. *Yikes.* That's not what I was looking for. Anyways, it's in the Old Testament book of Numbers, if you're interested.

Scrolling right along and—I found one. A *real* one. A biblical take on shrinking. I may or may not have done a happy dance when I read this golden nugget. Ready?

> *I take no pleasure in the one who shrinks back.*
> —Hebrews 10:38

Y'all. *I mean.*

Context matters, as always, but this verse has a straightforward backdrop. In the days of Moses, followers of God were severely persecuted. This particular scripture is addressing believers who took their suffering in stride. Who stood strongest in their conviction, confident in who they were. They'd lost their property and were thrown in prison, but they never shrank away from their truth: The God who made them would carry them through. That He created them for a purpose. That they could live boldly and not shrink away from who He made them to be.

Now, this isn't permission to fly off the handle. Which, frankly, I would appreciate. I have zero hesitation stepping up on a stage and sharing a piece of my mind. But the whole of God's Word would have me know that there is a godly kind of courage.

Scripture is chock-full of wisdom regarding mindfulness and self-control. It doesn't just matter what we say—it matters how and when we say it. Knowing when to keep your mouth shut isn't shrinking; it's expanding your maturity and your growth. We are called to live in authentic boldness, but what does that look like, biblically?

I'll tell you what I believe. It means raising our voice when it comes to the things that matter. Taking our steps in confidence when we know we are walking with God. It means that we don't retreat to our safe little shells when our messiness makes us feel vulnerable. God relishes those who don't shrink away, because He created us for a bold life.

When you pull back, you rob other people of knowing the fullness of your heart. Not only that, but you are robbing the world of who God made you to be. Your quirks, your courage, your ferocious sense of humor—all are inextricably part of your person. God put it in you, and He wants to use it. Aren't you tired of life in the shell?

• • • • • • •

I grew up drinking Grapico, which is a staple soft drink of the South. Actually, we don't really use the phrase *soft drink*; we literally call everything *coke*. I know it sounds weird, but if you want to try Grapico, this is what you have to do. Show up in the South and say, "I want a coke," at which point somebody will say, "Sure! What kind?" And *that* is when you say, "Grapico!" Trust me, you won't be disappointed.

When poured over ice, this purple elixir has an odd, fluffy blue fizz. Lord knows what nuclear chemical combo comes together to make this magic happen. I'm sure I'm drinking the equivalent of one of those elementary school volcano experiments. But I'm telling y'all, this drink is the greatest. It must be experienced to be understood.

When I moved to Florida, I couldn't find Grapico, and my fizz-loving heart was just broken. I pleaded with every grocery store manager I could to carry the product. I explained with impassioned detail the decadence of sipping fluffy blue fizz, and their response was, typically, horror.

Whatever; the magic isn't for everyone. Those managers are entitled to their wrong opinion. Grapico's weird is what makes it wonderful. It is a purple prince among cokes.

I've lived this Grapico-free Florida life for about six disappointing years. I mean, the sunshine and beaches are truly amazing. I do live in an endless summer.

But there are days when the sun leaves my body parched. When the heat beats down on my spirit. And when I open the fridge for a brisk refreshment, I miss my toxic blue fizz.

Let me be frank, because this truth stings just a little. There are some flavors that are so unique they'll be side-eyed by those who don't get it. You might be the juiciest peach in the world, but some people don't like peaches.

The hard truth is this: Rejection is part of the human experience. In a world as wildly diverse as this one, it's not possible to fit in at every table.

But the good news is, you don't have to. I'm serious about this.

Please hear me. It's not your responsibility to tone yourself down so you can fit in at somebody else's table. I'll wait a minute while you read that a few more times.

I feel so many of us need to hear that over and over again. We want to rally the troops around Grapico's greatness, when they really just *aren't gonna get it*. Your life goal shouldn't be to find the maximum number of people that prefer your flavor of human. Okay, Clarice, that came out far more Hannibal Lecter than I meant for it to, but still. You know what I mean.

You see, God isn't up in heaven with three different cookie cutters, stamping out humans and bringing us to life to be boring and homogeneous. No, friend. We were *fearfully and wonderfully* made—each and every one of us as unique as a fingerprint. The work of God is intentional. Don't you think that includes your quirks?

The tragic irony of trying to conform to the world by lessening who we are is that in an effort to avoid society's rejection, we are rejecting the very people that God created us to be.

Your authentic self, your weirdness, your silly jokes and bold personality—those are things that honor your Creator. Don't you dare shove it down inside.

I mean, sure. It's possible you might scare the crap out of some people. Your friends, your colleagues, maybe even your therapist. (Sorry, Dr. C.)

God created you in His image. There's a place for you at His table, in all of your quirky glory. Let your freak flag fly, friend. Step out and live in boldness. Laugh until you snort, keep your elbows on the table, lean deeply into who you are, and leave those emotional Spanx at home. Nobody has time for all that. God serves up a bounty of flavors and all sorts of swirly combos.

> God created you in His image. There's a place for you at His table, in all of your quirky glory.

At the end of the day other creatures (including humans) can be just as scared of me as I am of them. They can be just as nervous to show their soft underbelly as I am hesitant to show mine. But the only way we get to experience a deeper level of connectedness with each other, the only way we get to navigate the perilous waters of trust and friendship and growth, is by going into the water afraid. We can't continue to live life on the beach as memories get made in the water. The safety of that umbrella will never yield the joy of splashing in the waves.

This whole process gives me anxiety. I won't deny that fact. I hate even the smallest perceived rejection. The joke that leaves a room full of crickets. The text message that is left "on read." It's enough to make my stomach churn. But I know it's worth getting back in the water, over and over again. The reward of friendship—true, meaningful friendship—comes with an element of risk. Relationships are hard, but they become far less daunting if you remember that you aren't in this alone. I reveal my secrets; you reveal your quirks. I share that cheesy joke; you laugh loudly and unafraid. I'm scared and you're scared, and we can build something from there.

Come on in, friend. The water is fine.

> The only way we get to experience a deeper level of connectedness with each other, the only way we get to navigate the perilous waters of trust and friendship and growth, is by going into the water afraid.

CHAPTER 8

TWO TRUTHS AND A LIE

The greatest thing you'll ever learn is to love and be loved in return.

—Eden Ahbez, "Nature Boy"

When I was in eighth grade, I was voted "best dressed."

I earned this distinction by wearing crisp collared shirts layered beneath V-neck sweaters with flare-cut jeans and platform shoes.

Top half: Mr. Rogers. Bottom half: disco queen.

Cross my heart, this was fashionable at the time, and I wasn't given the honor ironically. What was ironic, though, is that none of the clothes I wore in eighth grade actually belonged to me.

They belonged to a girl named Christa, who was a blue-eyed beauty with an easy demeanor that naturally drew folks in.

Christa was honey, and our classmates were flies, and that had been the case for as long as I could remember. Eventually, in high school, she would go on to become homecoming queen, but that wasn't a thing in eighth grade. So instead, she was voted "class favorite," which, of course, is the eighth grade equivalent of the Queen of Everything. And because our school determined that you could only be given one superlative, the honor of "best dressed" was passed along to me: the daughter of a financially strapped single mother, wearing Christa's hand-me-down clothes.

Talk about imposter syndrome.

Let me tell you how this all came about. I'd known Christa ever since I was a kid, when my family moved to Dothan, Alabama. We both attended First Baptist Church and were pleasant in a Sunday school kind of way, but we'd never been what you would call friends.

Not that I hadn't tried. I had wanted to be in Christa's circle ever since fifth grade, when I realized we rode the same bus to school. I say "realized" because for the first half of that year, she and her clique hid from me behind a giant azalea bush every morning until the bus arrived.

Looking back now, I wonder what particular thing I had done to freak them out so much. Was it the way I sang "The Phantom of the Opera" at the top of my lungs on the street corner? Or the way I occasionally stooped down and shouted "Hello!" into storm drains, hoping a Ninja Turtle might one day respond? Or perhaps it was the way I would delicately relocate bugs from the center of the road to the grass (God forbid they get hit by a car).

Whatever the girls' reasons may have been, they were

eventually forced out of hiding. As it turned out, one of their mothers was my Sunday school teacher, and when she caught wind of their mean girl shenanigans, she sat them down for a lecture on kindness.

"Girls, let me ask you something. Did our Lord Jesus hide behind a bush when that harlot was thirsty at the well?"

"No, Miss Ann."

"He certainly did not! And if Jesus can show kindness to a harlot, then the three of you can be sweet to that strange little girl at the bus stop."

"Yes, Miss Ann."

At least that is how I imagined the conversation going in my head.

Truth is, I don't have a clue as to what Miss Ann said that day, but she was always using that harlot story at church, so chances are good she worked it in. Anyway, whatever she said must have been compelling, because smack dab in the middle of the school year, I had three new friends chatting me up at the bus stop. I couldn't believe my luck.

Having been the weird kid for the better part of elementary school, I was tragically encouraged by this small kindness. It pains me to tell you this next part. One day after school, I hopped off the bus and ran straight into the house. I pulled out the phone book and looked up Christa's phone number. Then I gathered up every bit of my awesome, awesome social skills and dialed her number.

And holy cow, she answered.

"Hey, Christa! It's Mary Katherine!"

"Mary…Katherine?"

"Yes, your friend from the bus stop! I just wanted to let you know that for my eleventh birthday, my dad gave me a huge stuffed horse. It's so big that you can put a pillow on its back, and it looks just like a saddle. You could ride it like a real, live horse if it was alive, which it isn't, but anyways—guess what? I named it Christa. After you! Isn't that great?"

For some strange reason, that phone call didn't have the effect that I intended.

For the rest of that year, the girls were friendly at the bus stop, but if I saw them in the hallway at school, they would smile and wave and then fluidly redirect, like a school of fish encountering a questionable sea creature.

Looking back, I don't remember being hurt by this rejection. I'm not even sure I saw it as that. Instead, I was more like a golden retriever, happy to take an occasional bone. I spent fifth grade in the outskirts of a tight-knit circle of friends, hoping one day it would open up and include me. Sadly, it never did.

A few years later, my mother escaped an abusive second marriage and moved our family into an adorable little cottage. Wouldn't you know, our precious new home was directly across the street from Christa's. It was the summer before eighth grade, and Momma had been drinking coffee in the driveway, discussing carpooling logistics with Christa's momma. Two days before school started, it was decided that they would team up and divide those responsibilities. And just like that, Christa and I were placed into each other's orbit again.

Blessedly, this time was different. We had both grown up a little and regularly attended youth group together. I didn't walk around singing Broadway tunes or yelling into storm drains anymore. It seemed like the awkwardness of the Stuffed Horse Phone Call had worn off. At least, Christa never brought it up. She also didn't hide from me behind bushes anymore. That part was especially nice.

Due to convenience or compatibility, I can't know for sure, but over the next year, our relationship began to grow. Monday through Friday, we would chatter like birds all the way to school. Eventually, we shared more than conversation. I'd give her a piece of my gum; she'd lend me an American Eagle sweater. We'd review flash cards and stress over cheerleading tryouts (we both made the squad). Then we'd arrive at Carver Middle School, hop out of the car, and go our separate ways.

After years of being lonely and feeling like an outsider, I was thrilled to have her company. I never tried to clarify our friendship or push it beyond what it was. But sometimes clarity comes, whether you like it or not, and in eighth grade that lesson came for me the very last day of school.

It was yearbook signing day, which I recall felt like a strangely sad party. Books were distributed at the beginning of first period, and for the remainder of the day, inside jokes and sappy musings were scribbled on every page.

"Hey, MK!" a fellow cheerleader hollered across the classroom. "Come and sign my yearbook!"

I grabbed my glitter gel pen and made my way to her desk. I flipped open her book, uncapped my pen and—

"*No!*" she said, blocking me from writing my name. "Not there! That's my reserved page. You know, for my best friend."

"Oh," I said, more than a bit taken aback. I hadn't noticed the squiggly frame she'd drawn around the page, or the name scrawled across the top. "Sorry about that," I muttered, scribbling a quick message before closing the book.

I hoped this wasn't an actual thing, but over the course of the afternoon I learned that it was. Over and over again, I'd reach my pen down to sign another yearbook. Over and over again I would be interrupted.

"Oh, don't sign there! You can't sign there. That page is reserved."

Not wanting to feel left out, I also reserved a page for my very best friend. I collected signatures and made sure to direct people away from that holy, protected space.

When the final bell rang that day, I jumped in the back seat of my momma's van, Christa beside me as we carpooled home. Christa and I exchanged yearbooks, and before I even had a chance to direct her toward that dedicated space, she scribbled something short and sweet on the corner of some random page. It only took a second for me to realize there was barely an inch of blank space left in her entire yearbook, so I uncapped my silver gel pen, found a blank corner, and did the same.

When I got home, I threw my backpack on the floor and shoved the yearbook onto the back of some random shelf. In it, a silvery-framed page remained: forever unsigned and reserved for a very best friend.

What I would like to tell you is that the very next year, I made several new friends and—*tralala!*—I immediately recovered from that middle school heartache. But that would only be half true. The fact is, I did go to high school and magically found my crew of fellow goat thieves (that's a story for another day). But the wounds of rejection didn't exactly disappear.

In fact, twenty years later, I found myself sitting in front of my therapist, baffled as to why stories from an elementary school bus stop and a middle school yearbook were suddenly pouring out of me. I had scheduled the appointment to work through some loneliness related to Ian and I relocating to Fort Myers, Florida. Building community is a hard thing to do— and I found it to be much harder with a toddler at home and a baby on the way. I was feeling like that awkward new girl all over again.

Eventually, I found a church to plug in to. Every weekend, I dressed up and attempted small talk with every person who half-way smiled at me. I couldn't help but feel like a hot mess puppy with a helicopter tail, begging in an animal shelter: *Please love me! Please, please, love me!*

There were four women in my Sunday school class who I couldn't help but adore. I hoped one day they would notice my tragic enthusiasm and have some social pity. Invite me to a play date, or coffee, or *anything.*

Everything about them seemed so casual and confident: their clothes, their friendships, their parenting. They were the kind of friends who passed pieces of gum to one another during Big Church and giggled as the crinkling wrappers drew side-eye from the older, blue-haired ladies.

They were clearly a tight-knit circle, but they made room for me at Mothers of Preschoolers and in Sunday school. We shared prayer requests and swapped babysitters' phone numbers. Once or twice, they casually dropped the idea of "getting our husbands together for a cookout." But then, whenever the weekend passed, they would post pictures of girls' lunches and kids' birthday parties and backyard cookouts with the husbands. All seemingly wonderful events to which I had not been invited.

As a grown woman, I felt so utterly ridiculous. Watching those women congregate in the parking lot after church made me feel so sad and resentful. And that's how I found myself back in the therapist's chair, unloading about all of the things: Broadway singing, V-neck sweaters, Ninja Turtles, and yearbook signatures.

"Wow, I'm sorry," I said, wiping my cheeks dry. "This is so embarrassing."

"Nothing embarrassing about sadness," Dr. C assured me.

"I know. It's just…I can't believe I am still so affected by all of this. I'm an adult. It's been two decades! Why am I still so angry?"

"Hmm," Dr. C replied. "Who are you angry at?"

I knew this question was rhetorical, yet I hoped Dr. C would do the work of unpacking it for me. But no. He just leaned back in his chair and got comfortable with my silence.

In moments like that, I sometimes wonder if Dr. C feels the way I do when I watch my four-year-old eat noodles with a fork. It's uncomfortable to watch her struggle through that process. She is so awkward and inefficient. Sometimes I just want to reach across the table, twirl the freaking fork, and shove the dang noodles in her mouth.

I could save her so much time, but then, what would she learn?

The hamster wheel in my brain picked up speed.

Who *was* I mad at?

Was it Christa? It's not like she'd done anything wrong. If I was being honest, it's what she hadn't done that made me feel so upset. She hadn't thought to go to that special reserved space in my yearbook. She hadn't thought of reserving a special place for me. Because after all that time, and all those talks, she didn't consider me her best friend.

But I realized that wasn't her fault. And I wasn't really mad at Christa.

So was I mad at the other women in my church? I wanted so badly to be a part of their circle but never quite made it in. Wasn't I funny? Wasn't I sweet? Wasn't I the kind of girl that people wanted to have around?

"I am mad at myself," I said out loud. It was a revelation. Not so much for Dr. C, who I assumed already knew this. I needed to test the idea on my tongue, to see if it felt true. And while it didn't really make much sense for me to be angry with myself, I knew it was exactly how I felt.

"You are mad at yourself for…?" Dr. C asked.

I breathed in deep to steady myself.

"I'm mad at myself for being unlovable," I responded.

The emotional weight of that realization swallowed the rest of our session whole. There was no point in diving into anything else; we had found the bleeder. The work of healing a lifelong wound had finally just begun.

Like so many other wounds to the soul, I discovered that my lasting pain wasn't from the initial injury, which was honestly pretty small. And being married to an ER doctor, I've learned this is the way of things: A wound can seem so small and harmless at first, but if it's ignored and untreated? Well, even the tiniest opening can allow something more nefarious to slip in.

Doubt had infected my spirit. It found the wound of young social rejection and slipped in through that partially open door. It was a voice that whispered, "You're too much" and "You're not enough," all at once, in a confusing, twisty lie.

Turns out, Christa wasn't trying to say I was unlovable. That was my doubt. The women at church weren't trying to tell me that I was unwanted. That was also my doubt. And even though the message sort of made sense to me, in that it would at least give context to a history of social struggles, that didn't make it true.

• • • • • • •

Back on that same fifth grade bus all those years ago, there was a game the kids used to play. It was called Two Truths and a Lie. The goal was to make three statements (two true, one false) and ask others to solve the riddle.

For instance, I would say: *Where's the lie?*

1. Mrs. Cook is my science teacher.
2. I have a dog named Mac...and...
3. I am actually a princess, but my cousin stole the throne and that isn't my real mother, but a CIA bodyguard tasked with protecting my identity.

Okay, so I was terrible at this game. Mostly because I enjoyed telling fantastical lies. I didn't understand that the trick to a really good lie was to create one that actually made sense in the context of the truth. As it turns out, Satan is pretty much the best at this game. In my ear, a message was playing on repeat, and it sounded like this:

1. As a child, I had a hard time making friends.
2. At thirty-five, I had a hard time making friends... therefore...
3. I am unlovable.

Where's the lie?

Looking back, I want to reach my arms through time and wrap them around my awkward younger self. I want to tell her that it's okay to feel lonely, because making friends is a hard and humbling affair. But I also wanted to tell her to never give up trying. That authentic community requires sharing more than a few pieces of gum, and like a toddler over a plate of noodles, she would figure that part out over time.

But the thing I want to tell her most, with one hand on either side of her face, is this: We found the lie, MK. You were never unlovable. We are fearfully and wonderfully made—every awesomely awkward piece. And if someone isn't drawn to the parts of you that God made quirky, then, quite simply, those aren't your people. And that can hurt, because dadgummit, loneliness hurts.

But you were never, ever unlovable.

• • • • • • •

Sometimes we jump into Two Truths and a Lie without realizing we're playing the game. It's a reel of deep, unconscious thinking that plays in the depths of our minds. Now, I don't claim to be some kind of therapist, but I've invested some serious time in that chair. The patient side, sure, but I'd like to think that I've picked up some skills along the way. So let me play therapist for just one moment, with the disclaimer that, well, I'm not one.

What is a painful memory from your life? One that seriously left you limping?

Have you got one? That's one truth.

Now, think of another situation in your past that marked you, that cut you deep.

Got it? Okay, that's two.

And it's important to acknowledge these things as *truth*. That they happened and shouldn't be discounted. I think we can be tempted to minimize hurt just because it occurred a little while back. At the fifth grade bus stop or on eighth grade yearbook day. Or the guy who stood us up for the date. Or the work friend who threw you under the bus on that big collaborative project. We want to internally dismiss those things as silly in the grand scheme of our grown-up lives. But listen: Nothing that bruises us is silly or insignificant. And Satan will try to use all of it. He will take your hurtful history, your distrust, your doubt, and spin some masterfully calculated lies. For example:

Truth: Your extended family is a hot mess + Truth: Your parents' marriage fell apart = Lie: You won't have a happy family of your own.

See how it works? Satan's the best at this game. He lures you into seeing a future that repeats your heartaches of the past. And the worst part is, it seems pretty logical. In your mind, the math makes sense. Rejection plus rejection times rejection seems to equal being unlovable.

But that right there is a lie. The suffering you experience at the hands of others has nothing to do with your worth. It has to do with their own jagged edges bumping into your heart. In my best "therapist" voice, I want to lean forward and tell you: Your injuries aren't your fault. Other people's mess is other people's mess. You've always been lovable *and* loved.

There's another lie that Satan has had me tangled up in for years. Check it out:

Truth: We need friendship + Truth: We meet a likable person = Lie: This friendship is written in the stars.

Oof. Right?

I think it's part of our misunderstanding about community. Yes, we should be loving to everyone. Yes, they should be loving to us. In an ideal world, there wouldn't be cliques in the church and mean girls wouldn't own the PTA.

But truth is, as much as we are built for connection, it doesn't mean we'll have it with everyone. Nor is it their responsibility to always extend it to you and me. That was the hardest truth for my golden retriever heart to grasp. I meet people I like, and I get goofy and excited: *Please like me please like me please like me.* Maybe they will like me. Maybe they won't. Their feelings don't determine my worth.

Here's the way the math really is:

Truth: We need friendship + Truth: We meet a likable person = Truth: You aren't everyone's people and not everyone is your people, and that's okay. We can still love each other.

When I look at that truth, it helps me release others. I can release Christa, who, again, was so kind to me, but didn't see me as a best friend. Was that mean of her? No. But does it help me be kind to myself when I look at the truth of that hurt? Yes. It reminds me that I didn't fail in my friendship with Christa. And that whether or not I become someone's bestie has nothing to do with how lovable I am.

Those cute church moms that I wanted to click with so bad? I'm letting them off the hook, too. Even if it makes me sad. The funny part is, I'm sure there have been those along my path who have pursued a deeper friendship with me and I was left unaware. I'm sure sitting in my DMs right now is a message I've left unread. I can barely get my laundry sorted, much less my social media inbox. And it's not because I don't care. I do. But God created twenty-four-hour days, not thirty-six, not forty-two. That's another truth. And to love Ian and my family well, to keep our home running, to write this book, feed the cat, and occasionally wash my hair? That takes up almost every portion of those twenty-four-hour days. I have to use discretion when building relationships. It's good for others to do the same.

There are so many variables at play in our lives that we can be tempted to believe Satan's lies: That we are too messy or too weird to belong. That rejection means we are unlovable. Satan is shady, and his goal is to hurt us. There's a reason he's called the Deceiver.

But God wants our joy. His plans are good. We have to cling to *His* truth.

His Truth: You aren't just lovable—you are already *loved*.

And the best part? You don't have to earn it.

CHAPTER 9

FIND YOUR FELLOW GOAT THIEVES

You can't stay in your corner of the Forest waiting
for others to come to you. You have to go to them
sometimes.

—Winnie the Pooh

Are you sure this is the place?" Momma asked, incredulously.
We were parked front and center of a dilapidated
shopping center. A sign in the window read THE ROCK CHURCH,
but I had to admit it looked nothing like any church I'd ever
attended. A check-cashing business sat to the left, but other than
that, the building was vacant.

"Yep," I said, unbuckling my seat belt. "This is the place.
Pick me up at seven."

Momma raised an eyebrow. My proposed three-hour window was clearly stretching her comfort zone.

"I think I'll just park and wait," she murmured, eyes sweeping the desolate strip center, looking for a drug deal to go down.

"No, no, that won't be necessary," I replied. The thought of Momma in that parking lot by herself was a little too "beginning of a true crime documentary" for my taste.

"Anyways," I added, "Blount's dad is staying the whole time. I will call you as soon as we're done."

"Hm," she responded. "I guess that's okay. But wait a minute...Blount *Floyd*?"

No doubt, Momma knew this name as my opposition for eighth-grade class president. She'd seen me spend countless hours that year gluing safety pins to the backs of painted puzzle pieces—creating an adorable campaign button I could distribute around school. She heard how excited I was when those gold puzzle pieces became a vogue new accessory in the halls of Carver Middle School. She watched me practice my election day speech in front of the bathroom mirror.

When the big day arrived, both candidates, Blount and yours truly, got to address the school through our television broadcast system. And boy, was I ready. I waxed poetic on how our diverse student body was a beautiful picture comprised of unique pieces. How I believed every one of us was necessary to create this "bigger picture," and that we only needed to come together—*like a puzzle*—to accomplish great things. You could hear the applause in the hallway when my speech wrapped up.

I had it in the bag, for sure.

Then it was Blount's turn. He came on the screen with his baby-blue eyes, flashed a playful grin, and busted out the song from *Titanic*.

"Neeeeear, faaaar, whereEVER YOU ARE!" he screeched. The entire school was rolling with laughter. He won class president by a total of three votes.

"Yep, that's Blount," I acknowledged. "The only one in town, I imagine."

I grabbed my drumsticks and hopped out of the van, unsure of what I would encounter. Which, oddly enough, was the entire point of this endeavor: I was showing up. Putting myself out there. It's what I resolved to do when I got home from eighth grade yearbook signing day. I'd spent the rest of that afternoon beneath the covers of my bed as that godforsaken empty page taunted me from the back of a shelf. I desperately wanted to find my people, but I knew what that would require. The friendships that I craved couldn't be built with gossip and gum. I would have to be vulnerable. Take risks. Fish in deeper waters. Which is exactly why I accepted the invitation to audition for Blount's band. Earlier that week, he found me in the parking lot after school, waiting for my momma to arrive. He sat on the curb beside me to chat, in that cool-but-casual way that Blount managed to do just about everything.

"Hey, MK. You were pretty great in jazz band today. Have you ever thought about being in your *own* band?"

No, I hadn't thought about it, but I figured I'd give it a shot. No pain, no gain, or something, right?

I gave Momma a little shoo and then blew her a kiss and

walked inside. The church was one big room, with chairs placed in rows facing a platform stage. Blount's dad, Mr. Steve, had taken a seat in the very last row. The musicians were warming up their instruments.

"MK!" Blount shouted into a mic. "Yay! You made it!"

"Hey," I said, waving with my drumsticks. I walked to the front of the stage.

"Everybody, this is MK," Blount said to the group. "MK, this is everybody."

There were five kids standing on stage, strumming or fiddling with chords. Oliver was someone I had seen around since middle school, and he'd always been nice enough. We weren't friends, but we weren't *not* friends, either. His dad was pastor of the local Presbyterian church.

"Hey, MK! I'm Oliver," he said, tightening up a string. He chuckled. "But I guess you probably knew that."

Oliver's laugh was as warm as sunshine, and he reminded me of a Muppet. He was a big guy, but not in a football-playing sort of way. He had a thick head of sandy hair and a smile that covered his face. He wore a bright orange Veggie Tales shirt and, I couldn't help but notice, no shoes.

"Hey, MK!" Elliott waved, from his place behind the mic. *And there's the lead singer*, I thought to myself, because it made perfect sense. Elliott and I grew up at First Baptist together, and I'd heard him sing over the years, from children's chorus to praise band. He was talented, boisterous, and born to perform. He was another person I kinda knew, kinda didn't, but his presence settled my nerves a bit. I was glad for a familiar face.

There was one complete stranger standing in back of the stage, tuning her bass guitar. She was a tiny little thing who couldn't have weighed more than ninety pounds—a hundred if you included her hair. It was thick and brown and fell to her waist. A hunk of it was pushed forward over part of her face, and it seemed she was hiding behind it. She reminded me of a little wood nymph.

"Hi. I'm Kara," she said with a smile. "This is my dad's church." Her voice took me by surprise. It didn't match her tiny frame—it was deep and rich. Maybe even sultry. She sounded a little like Cher. If Cher was an adorable wood nymph.

"Nice to meet you," I replied, noting in my head that she was the second PK (pastor's kid) in the room; it felt like something I should keep in mind. Anytime you throw PKs in the mix, it ups your chance of serious shenanigans. That's science.

"Well," said Blount, addressing the group. "Y'all want to get this thing started?"

I took my seat behind the drums and Blount distributed folders. He told us which song we'd be starting with, and I opened it up on the stand.

Hm, that's weird.

I glanced around the stage to see if maybe I'd gotten the wrong folder. But nope. This was it. What everyone else was looking at. The sheet in front of me had no bars, no music, no nothing.

It was lyrics, y'all. Only. Lyrics.

Oh, my gosh, I thought to myself. *I have to make this up as I go?!*

My heart began to race. I'd only been in jazz band for half a semester. Before that, I was in marching band. And before that, I was beating on my desk with pencils and driving my sixth-grade English teacher crazy. Mrs. Ivey finally erupted: "Drum tryouts are happening in the music room. Please go now. You are driving me crazy." So, I traded my pencils for a pair of Vic Firths, and the next thing I knew, I was drumming. That being said, I had very little experience with freestyle performance, and even less confidence. But before I had a chance to freak out completely, Blount struck a power chord. And just like that, the room filled up with sound: Ollie was strumming, Kara was plucking, and Elliott jumped in, singing. Next thing I knew, my foot found the bass and we were making music. It was awkward and clunky and young, but it was *ours*.

Something magical happened in the Rock Church that afternoon. The five of us showed up as individuals, and together became something else entirely. We were all vulnerable and testing new ideas. It was scary and thrilling and collaborative.

I'd try something with the cymbals, and Blount would notice and smile. Elliott would hit a falsetto note and we'd all hoot and holler. Oliver would notice when a bandmate's confidence was waning, and he'd subtly pull them back in.

"Kara, could you harmonize that final chorus?" he'd say. "I bet that'd really bring it home."

By the time we reached the last song in our folder, a cohesive sound was emerging. Blount finished one final solo, and then let the last note ring.

Clapping came from the back of the church. At some point our parents had slipped in. It was nine p.m. and dark outside. We'd all been lost in the music.

"What about the name Soul Purpose?" I asked. "It's a play on words, you know? Like, our sole purpose is to glorify God… but we also have *soul*."

Blount laughed. "I don't hate it," he said.

Oliver smiled. "I dig it."

Elliott nodded his head, and Kara smiled amiably.

It was official: We had music and had a name. We were officially *a band*.

· · · · · · ·

Soul Purpose made a home in Blount's garage, where we practiced four days a week. Mr. Steve took note of which snacks we'd devour, and he kept the pantry stocked. At four o'clock, we'd grab a few Pop-Tarts, chat for a minute, then jam until somebody's momma called.

One day, after a few months of practice, Blount called us in for a chat.

"So, what do y'all think," he asked the group. "Are we ready for our first gig?"

There was a buzz of excitement among the band, and the consensus was *heck yes*, we were.

"Natalie Grant is playing the Farm Center next month, but she doesn't have an opening act. There's a competition for local bands to fill the spot…and I think we should enter."

"Do we need to use original songs?" Kara asked.

"For legal reasons, I think so," Blount responded.

"Do I have to wear shoes?" Oliver joked.

"At the Farm Center, Ollie? I think you're good," I laughed.

"We are gonna have to work our butts off," Elliott added.

"I agree. And write new songs," Blount said. "So…I'm thinking a songwriter's retreat. Who's in?"

As if he had to ask.

We piled in cars with suitcases, guitars, and notebooks, then rode to the lake for a three-day weekend. We were gonna write a platinum album. All we needed was time. The boys played guitar until their fingers bled, and the girls filled pages with lyrics. At the end of each day, we'd gather at the floating dock and compile what we had into songs.

What was intended as a song-building exercise became something else entirely. It turns out, you can't write original music without exposing a piece of who you are. A lyric here would point to a story there, and we'd end up talking for hours. One night, the floating dock was somehow unhitched from its post. After an hour of talking and writing, we found ourselves floating in the middle of open water.

It was fun for a while, singing under the stars, but around midnight, I started to panic. Kara and I made the boys jump in and tow us back to shore. I remember they looked like seahorses pulling a ginormous floating chariot. It was freaking hysterical. During the ride, I convinced Blount that sharks lived in Lake Martin, and I swear to you, his body levitated out of the water and onto that dock, and we all laughed until we cried.

When Monday finally came, the band went home with so much more than music. Not only were we ready to take on our first gig, but together, we could take on the world.

• • • • • • •

The morning of the Natalie Grant contest, the band found a quiet hallway behind the auditorium. Hundreds of people had taken their seats, and we were a collective nervous wreck. We decided we could use some prayer, so we huddled up, bowed our heads, and…

"Excuse me, are you Soul Purpose?" a sweaty man with a clipboard asked.

"Yes," Blount replied. "That's us."

"Hi, everyone. I'm Tom. Three bands scratched last minute, and y'all are coming up next. I need you to fill out some paperwork, so I can announce your act."

"We are…*next?*" Elliott asked, panic plain on his face. Kara scooted close to his side and patted him on the back.

Tom handed Blount the clipboard, and hovered over us, expectantly. Prayer was gonna have to wait. We gathered to look at the form.

ACT ANNOUNCEMENT FORM
Band Name: Soul Purpose
Band Members: Blount, Kara, Elliott, Oliver, and
Mary Katherine
Song Name: 24/7
Band Verse:
Why this verse?:

"Um, guys…" Blount said.

"Yeah?"

"We're supposed to have a band Bible verse. And a good reason for why we chose it."

"Oh, heck," Oliver said. "I've got a really good one. Dad preached on it last weekend. Let me think…"

"Better hurry," I said. The band on stage was taking a bow.

"We could always go with John 3:16. That's safe," Elliott added.

"No, no," Oliver shook his head. "It was really awesome. And it was verse 24:7, which we could totally use."

Tom not-so-subtly leaned in toward the group.

"Y'all about ready?" he asked.

"I remember!" Oliver said. "It's Job 24:7. It's something about following the heart of God. Tell them we chose it because we want to live it out, 24/7."

"Oh, I love that," I piped in.

Blount scribbled down the answers and handed the clipboard to Tom.

"Good luck, kids," he said over his shoulder, as he jogged out of the room.

"Soul Purpose to the stage, Soul Purpose to the stage."

"We've got this," Blount said with confidence. "Purpose on three?"

We put our hands together and chanted on three, then made our way to the side of the stage and waited to be announced.

"MK," Kara whispered to me. "What verse did the band pick? I had to run to the bathroom and didn't get to hear."

"Something in Job, I think," I said.

"Hm. That's an interesting choice," she replied.

Tom walked up to the mic, and we all squeezed hands one more time.

"And now, introducing Soul Purpose!" he said. The crowd

applauded as we took to the stage. We were the youngest competitors by far, and they seemed to love us already.

"Soul Purpose has chosen the verse Job 24:7," Tom said, opening his Bible.

"Job 24:7 says…" He paused for a moment, seeming confused. "It says…"

He looked back at Oliver, who grinned and gave a thumbs-up.

"Okay," Tom continued. "Job 24:7: Lacking clothes, they spent the night naked; they have nothing to cover themselves in the cold."

Oh no. I wanted to melt into the floor, but Tom wasn't done yet.

"The band chose this scripture because they want to live it out 24/7! Ladies and gentlemen—Soul Purpose!"

• • • • • • •

"C'mon y'all. It wasn't that bad," Kara said, plucking her bass.

The band was back in Blount's garage, but nobody wanted to play.

"It was my fault, everyone. I'm sorry I messed up the verse." Oliver was hanging his head, now, and nobody wanted to see that.

"Well, I thought it was hilarious," Blount said with a shrug. "But we probably won't get booked for a while."

Elliott didn't say a thing. He just patted Oliver's back.

"Well," I said, breaking the silence. "I have some happy news. Believe it or not, we've just been booked…for the National Peanut Festival!"

Dothan, Alabama, is a farming town that takes peanuts very seriously. There's literally a giant golden peanut in front of our city's welcome center. Booking the festival was primo, and the band was ecstatic.

"What?" said Kara. "No way!"

"Yep," I replied with a smile. "I just got the email yesterday. And we've got three weeks to prepare for it, so…"

"Plug in, everybody!" yelled Blount. "We've got work to do."

• • • • • • •

The stage we were assigned at the festival was a decent piece of real estate. It was just off the main drag, beside a life-sized peanut that waved as visitors arrived. The seats filled up a good half hour before we were slated to begin. There were professional lights and a designated sound guy. We felt like the World's Biggest Deal. When Blount kicked off with a solo riff, the crowd jumped out of their seats. For the next ninety minutes, we played our hearts out, and they never sat back down.

"That. Was. Awesome!" Kara yelled as we jumped backstage for intermission.

"Oh, we killed it!" Elliott agreed. High-fives and hugs were passed around.

"We still have another hour until our next set. Who wants to check out the fair?" I asked.

Elliott and Blount decided to join, while the others grabbed corndogs and cokes. We took a quick picture with the waving peanut, then walked the main drag to our next adventure.

"Look, y'all! A petting zoo! *Awww*, we just have to!" I pleaded.

"Okay, MK," laughed Elliott. "But you can't take anything home."

There were at least fifty animals in a tiny corral, and the attraction stunk of manure. There was a single carnival worker inside, whose job seemed to be twofold: to convince all the parents to purchase cereal at a dollar a handful, and to supervise children who were feeding the animals so that nobody lost a finger.

I was feeding a blimp-sized pony when I noticed a little black goat. It was staying in the center of the little corral, away from the grabby hands of children.

"Look at that little guy right there," I said to Blount. "He is *so* over this."

We both laughed. Who could blame him? Stale cereal and screaming children had to get old after a while. The Shetland pony nibbled my fingers, then turned to trot away. I wiped my hands on the side of my jeans and was just turning to leave...and then it happened.

I felt like I was watching in slow motion as the carnival worker raised his hand. Then, with as much force as he could muster, he struck the goat on his little behind, causing him to fall forward.

"*Get!*" he yelled, using his boot to kick him back toward the fence.

I tried to scream in protest, but my mouth couldn't form the words. My heart had felt every blow.

"Blount," I said, wiping my tears.

"No," he replied.

"Please," I pleaded. "We have to do something."

Blount looked at Elliott for backup, but Elliott shrugged. "I'm Team MK with this one."

"Fine," said Blount, shaking his head, like he couldn't believe what he was saying. "We can do something, but we have to be smart about it."

The three of us devised a plan, and it went something like this: Elliott would get in line for cereal and keep the carnival worker distracted by asking him lots of pointless questions. Blount would stand on the opposite side, serving as backup diversion. And I would grab the goat.

Elliott did a fantastic job, asking a hundred-odd questions. His pocket of change bought two handfuls of cereal, and just the right amount of time. Blount motioned for me to hurry along, but the goat was flat out uncatchable. I hung my body over the rail and reeeeached.

Got him.

In one swift motion, I grabbed his horn and tugged him toward the fence. Then I took a deep breath, grabbed the goat, and ran like hell. Out to the main drag, toward the waving peanut, I sprinted as hard as I could. I was terrified to look behind me, but Blount was back there, somewhere.

"Go! Go! Go!" he cheered me on, cackling as he ran. I would later find out he was laughing this way because I carried the goat like a toddler. His little body was facing mine, as I clung to the bottom half. His front legs were dangling over my back, and his head peeped over my shoulder. I darted across the thoroughfare toward the waving peanut.

"Excuse me!" I yelled, crossing in front of a family.

"Nice goat!" the father hollered back, as if this were perfectly normal.

I arrived at the tent, covered in sweat and smelling like a zoo. The crowd was arriving for our next set, so the goat and I headed straight backstage.

Kara and Oliver were sitting on a blanket, surrounded by a smorgasbord of food. I set the goat down and doubled over, trying to catch my breath.

"Will…y'all…make…sure…he doesn't run away?" I panted.

Kara immediately attended the goat, who nibbled her hand for a treat.

Oliver only giggled and took a bite of his funnel cake.

"MK," Kara said, rubbing the goat between his ears. "Do I even want to know?"

"Nope," said Blount, joining the group. "Don't incriminate yourself, Kara-bear."

He looked at his watch, then the goat, then back to his watch again.

"All right, MK. You got your goat. Congratu-freaking-lations. Now, I don't know what your plan for Little Dude is, but you've got fifteen minutes to figure it out. We have to finish our set."

"Barnaby," I replied, finally catching my breath. "His name is Barnaby."

But Blount was already back onstage, tuning up his guitar.

I looked at Barnaby, who was perfectly content, getting pets from the band. He was a chill little goat, all things considered. But I still couldn't leave him backstage. What if he wandered away? What if he got captured? I couldn't let him go back to a life of abuse and misery.

"Ollie," I said in a sugary voice. "Can you help me get Barnaby out to the car?"

· · · · · · ·

Oliver and I hopped back onstage with about a minute to spare. Kara was already behind her bass, and Elliott was warming his voice. I took my seat and twirled my sticks, centering my mind on the music.

"Psst…" Elliott turned his head, leaning away from the mic. "I put the rest of those Lucky Charms in your purse."

Then he turned to the mic, hyped up the crowd, and counted off our next song.

· · · · · · ·

When we finished our last set, I asked Blount if he'd pack up my drums. He sighed and begrudgingly agreed to help. I gave him a ginormous hug.

"I'm just worried about Barnaby," I explained. "He never finished his dinner."

I spotted Momma's car across the lot and beeped the Unlock button.

Please be okay please be okay please be okay please—

Barnaby's little head popped up in the back seat. I had been wrong to worry about Barnaby. He was more than okay. In fact, he finished his dinner. Apparently, Barnaby didn't love cereal, which explained his disinterest at the petting zoo. What he *did* love to eat was literally everything else, including but not limited to: leather interior, a center console, parts of three seat belts, and every single interior door handle.

"Oh, *no*," I said aloud, the blood draining from my face. "Momma's gonna kill me."

When I got home from the Peanut Festival, Momma was already asleep. I was exhausted, too, but couldn't sleep until Barnaby was somewhere safe and secure. The car had been a terrible choice. Maybe he was claustrophobic?

I put Barnaby out on our screened-in porch and went to bed to pray.

Dear God, please don't let Momma kill me. Amen.

• • • • • • •

"Mary Katherine Samples!"

I awoke to Momma screaming my name, which honestly, she didn't do often. She was spitting nails, which was to be expected. I figured she'd discovered her car.

But no. Not yet.

What she'd discovered was Barnaby, standing in the dining room, chewing a piece of screen door. He had spent the entire night roaming our house and pooping out last night's dinner. As angry as Momma already was, she wasn't aware that his dinner had been the inside of her car.

I immediately started crying, begging Momma for mercy.

Barnaby was an abuse case! He was beaten and kicked! I couldn't let him go on like that!

I walked Momma out to the car and waited for her to explode. Instead, she went cold, dead silent. She left the car and walked inside and stopped in the middle of the doorway. Barnaby was now on the dining room table, proud as a little mountain goat.

She looked at Barnaby, then back at me, then again at Barnaby.

And then, she did the scariest thing I've ever seen Momma do: She started laughing.

Oh my gosh, I've done it, I thought. *I've actually broken Momma.*

In between laughter and pouring tears, Momma pointed to Barnaby.

"Mary Katherine," she said, clearing her throat. "You have one hour to get that goat out of this house. One. Hour."

"Yes, ma'am."

"And don't you ever, *ever*, do this again. Do you hear me?"

"Yes, ma'am. Wait…You mean don't rescue any animals—or just goats specifically?"

"Never. Again."

"Got it. Yes, ma'am. Never again."

I called the band and filled them in.

"I'm serious, y'all. It's an *emergency*," I said. "I have to find Barnaby a home. Quick. I think I broke my Momma."

Kara knew of a farm near her house, which she drove past every day. They'd recently put a sign on the property advertising goats for sale. If we could somehow get Barnaby over the fence…

"I can help," Oliver said. Elliott was in, as well.

"If y'all drive to the parking lot of Dobbs BBQ, I can show you the rest of the way," Kara said.

"It's a plan," Blount declared. "I'll drive. Oliver, Elliott, y'all head over to MK's house. Kara, we'll see you in thirty."

We followed Kara down a country road, then pulled off on a wide, grassy shoulder. The sign was there, just as she said: GOATS 4 SALE with a phone number to call. The band piled out on the side of the road: five kids and a goat on a leash. Barnaby seemed confused by real grass, and cautiously nibbled a bit.

"I bet he's used to cereal," Elliott said. "He's in for a little adjustment."

"More than a little," Blount laughed. "Look at the other goats!"

The goats at the farm were solid brown and had floppy rabbit-like ears. Barnaby was black, except one little spot, and he had ears that stood up on his head.

"Well," said Oliver, stepping close. "Let's get this goat on the road."

The band gave Barnaby a pat and a hug, then took off his collar and leash. Ollie lifted him up, barely clearing the fence. Things were a little squirrely on the release, and Barnaby landed with a thud. But he hopped right up, shook like a dog, and trotted away toward the herd. When the other goats spotted him, they stopped chewing and stared.

Suddenly, I felt anxious for Barnaby. This was a whole new world. Did he have a clue how different he was? Would they accept him as part of the herd?

Barnaby presented himself with a *baa* that was so small it melted my heart. The others responded with curious sniffs, then seemed to lose interest entirely. It couldn't have been more than two or three minutes before the goats were grazing together. I'm not gonna lie, a piece of me felt emotional about the whole thing. The herd had accepted the misfit. Everything turned out okay.

As the band piled into the back of Blount's truck, I took a moment to soak in their laughter. These were people who loved me well and knew me for the misfit that I was. If I had to pilfer a petting zoo, then they'd be my partners in crime. There was never a question of if they'd show up; it was only a matter of how.

After years of being an outsider, desperate to belong, I finally had the type of friends you reserve a yearbook page for. The funny thing is, in our four years together, I never got around to making a special page for my fellow goat thieves to sign.

Maybe we shared too many secrets, too many adventures to squeeze into one small page. The memories and music just wouldn't make sense in the context of those small margins. How can you explain in written words the way it feels to be part of a fold? Vulnerability is a high-risk game, and so often it ends in rejection. I remember the ache of being an outsider, but I continued to put myself out there. And thank goodness, too, because some of the sweetest moments in all my life were born from one single risk. I was a nervous girl trying out for a band, looking to make a few friends. What I found was so much more than I could ever imagine.

I had found *my people.* The ones who would never hide behind the azaleas. Who saw my weird and thought it was wonderful. Who reciprocated vulnerability, support, and unconditional love. They were my partners in crime, and my fellow goat thieves. They were more than worth the wait.

• • • • • •

Can I tell you something? Something that took me sixteen years to learn? And if I'm being honest, I still have to relearn occasionally?

It's this: If you've ever felt lonely on the outskirts of a circle that just doesn't seem to be letting you in—walk away. You will find—or make—a new circle. If you want to make those precious friendships—the ones that deserve their own yearbook page—you have to stop chasing relationships with people whose circle is closed. Maybe they are too distracted with their lives to make room for a new relationship. Maybe they are in a social funk, or maybe they simply don't get you. That's not on you, my friend. Don't you dare water yourself down to be palatable for others. You are freaking fabulous—find a circle that sees it. Don't lose an ounce of energy hard-selling Grapico to people who don't get its greatness. There are folks all around you who feel lonely as well. Folks who *adore* blue fizz. But if you're too busy staring down the "it kid" circle, you might miss what's in front of your eyes.

Who knows where your people are going to come from. Finding friends isn't like shopping for hats. You don't breeze through Target with a shape and color in mind and leave with the perfect fit. Best friend hearts come in all sorts of packages. Look around, then look a little harder. That quiet girl from Sunday school who always has a book in her purse. You wouldn't believe the way she cuts loose when somebody suggests karaoke. That surgeon's wife who seems perfectly unapproachable, with her platinum blond hair and zillion-dollar purse? She's a Disney nerd. I'm not even kidding—she knows every word to *The Lion*

King. I've met them both and shocked myself at the wonderful friendships we forged.

You have to take risks to meet your fellow goat thieves, and they may not be who you expected. So, put your "perfect hat" standards aside for a while. You've heard about judging a book by its cover; well, don't go judging a soul by its skin suit. It's going to take courage to put yourself out there, and you'll probably strike out a few times. But trust me, dear one. It's worth the hard days. A true friend is better than silver. Your fellow goat thieves are out there, just waiting for you.

Go find them and love them well.

CHAPTER 10

ANNIVERSARY RATS

Keep your eyes wide open before marriage, half shut
afterwards.

—Benjamin Franklin

It's been said that my husband and I got married young, dumb,
and poor.

And it's true. I'm the one who said it.

Frankly, he wouldn't disagree, but we've made it to the other
side, and so far, we are still kicking. All's well that ends well,
right? Or I guess when it comes to marriage, all's well that...
doesn't end?

One of the most epic stories from our naïve early days
occurred when my husband called his mother to let her know
that he had found The One.

Back then, Ian was so (understandably) infatuated with me

that he was bursting at the seams to tell someone. So, with a heart full of love and a stomach full of butterflies, he picked up the phone and called his mom.

At two o'clock in the morning.

Understandably, the woman who was still paying the power bill for her college student son was decidedly not here for this update. Suzi, the woman who would ultimately become my mother-in-law, waited for Ian to catch his breath, which took a few minutes, and by that time she was thoroughly ruffled.

"You're getting married? That's wonderful, son. But where are y'all going to live? What are y'all going to eat? How are you going to pay for your car, your cell phone, and your rent?"

Ian was deeply offended by his mother's lack of immediate enthusiasm. He huffed with exasperation and said:

"*Gah*, Mom! I thought you would understand! All you need is *love!*"

(I swear to you I couldn't make this up if I tried.)

About one year later, I walked down the aisle in a three-hundred-dollar dress, holding some flowers my Momma picked out of a local bank's front lawn. Ian had a little-boy haircut, a red silk cummerbund, and eyes only for me. The pianist played "Jesus Loves Me" (yes, the one you sing in Sunday school), and both of our families cried.

Ian and I were two happy idiots; it was us against the world. So, with our bank accounts empty and the bills piling up, I took on a waitressing job at a local barbecue joint named Dreamland. As newlywed students without two dimes to rub together, love was *literally* all we had. We hoped it was going to be enough.

We took off for our honeymoon the following Saturday with

an envelope of cash (thanks to my waitressing tips) and a free place to stay (thanks to a family timeshare).

All in all, things were looking good.

I was so freaking excited to have a brand-new husband trapped in the car. He was my conversation hostage. I was still in that whole "I just want to know you mooooore" phase of love, which was made one hundred percent crazier by my newly minted last name.

I was a misses. Or was it mizrez?

Whatever, I was a wife. And not just any wife. I was Ian's wife! I just couldn't wait to know him, heart, mind, and soul—*AWWWW!!!*

Two bags of chips and a car nap later, we started chatting about American politics. To be honest, I have no idea where that conversation took a turn, but it took a hard freaking turn, and the next thing you know, the Backstroms were pulled over at a rest stop somewhere east of Boondock, Georgia.

Look, there's MK! Storming across the parking lot, yelling.

"I'll never have your liberal <bleeping> babies!"

And there's Ian. Stepping out of a car that still had JUST MARRIED painted across the back. Trailing after his hysterical bride as an entire row of truckers watched, laughing.

Hot. Mess.

This was the day my husband was given some insight into what a love language is. He tried to woo me back to the car with handpicked flowers. Gifts are not my love language. He tried to hold my hand and hug it out. Physical touch is not my love language. That poor guy went through the entire gambit, trying to figure out what my love language was. Acts of service, nope.

Words of affirmation, nope. Honeybun and a Diet Coke, nope. Apology?

Too soon, not enough, not accepted. Nope.

It turned out, in the early years of our relationship, my love language was being the center of attention, which isn't actually a love language. It's just an unhealthy form of codependency that, when nurtured, results in a very bratty wife and a tired, resentful husband. Didn't I tell you we were young and dumb? Yeah. It got worse before it got better.

A few months later, Ian and I moved into the basement apartment of my sister's house. It had one tiny bedroom over-looking a deck, which was lovely. But the bathroom was the size of a porta-potty, and that wasn't the greatest. I had to wash my hair with my elbows tucked—the shower was that small. But we could afford it, and since it turned out that love *wasn't* enough to pay all of our bills, into the basement we went.

Now, maybe it was the lack of sunshine or the fact Ian was applying to medical school, but at some point during the Year of the Basement Apartment, he decided that what he *really* needed to be happy and sane was a puppy. (It turns out that just having a wife around gets exhausting after a while.) Now, this obviously made perfect sense in our twenty-two-square-foot apartment, which is why my sister said no, and I said no, and literally any-one else he tried to convince said *no*.

But my scientist husband, undeterred by a two-woman veto, began a researching quest to find a small, easy-to-care-for pet that his sister-in-law and wife would approve. Now, if you ask Ian, this was the manifestation of some God-given wild-at-heart spirit within him, longing for a way to express itself. He needed something fresh and exciting. He needed life to stay shiny and adventurous. What he needed was—wait for it—a rat.

"No," I said.

"But they are among the smartest and cleanest of pets!" Ian pleaded.

"Absolutely not," I responded.

"But they can learn tricks, babe! I watched a video of this one rat that stored little beans in a match box. He would get them out any time he wanted a snack!"

"Oh, baloney. What kind of beans can fit in a freaking matchbox?"

"That's not the point!"

"The answer is *no*!"

Ian walked out onto the deck without saying a word and shut the door behind him. I almost followed, but I figured it was best to leave him be. He was probably mourning his lack of rat. He just needed a moment of peace, right?

Perhaps that was the mistake I made. I exited an argument with an *assumed* victory, when my husband never actually conceded. The surrender gene is recessive in the Backstrom family. It's just not a thing they do.

Oh, I should have seen the red flags flying. There was a zero percent chance that Ian had let this one go. But that is something I know *now*, after fifteen years of marriage.

It is not a thing I knew back then.

• • • • • • •

July 29, 2007

A group of servers were crowded around the drink station at Dreamland, chatting. It was a slow week, and our sections were mostly empty, except for an elderly woman in a corner booth waiting on her lunch. We took turns sipping Diet Mountain Dew from paper cups and exchanging whatever gossip we had to share. Which wasn't a lot. Slow week in more ways than one.

"Oh!" I smiled. "Today is mine and Ian's one-year anniversary!"

"Awww!" the girls sang in unison. "What do you think he's gonna give you?"

Crap. I hadn't really thought about that.

"Y'all, I have no idea!" I said. "What are you supposed to do the first year?"

None of us college kids had a clue, but that sweet old lady eating a rib sandwich did. Her name was Doris, and she informed us that your first anniversary is the year of paper, which could be a card, or money, or origami. As long as it's paper, you're good.

"I recommend a card with a coupon in it." Doris smiled, with a hunk of pork stuck between her front teeth.

"A coupon?" I asked.

"For something he *enjooooys*," she added with a little shimmy. I about fell over dead.

"Goodness. *Oh.* All right, Ms. Doris. I'll think on that," I said, filling up her sweet tea and ignoring the servers who cackled behind me. My face was hot as a poke. I dropped off her check, cashed out my tips, and asked the manager if I could duck out early.

I needed to escape my coworkers' coupon jokes. I'd be hearing them for the next month, at least. And anyways, I had two hours to figure out how to make paper convey my everlasting love to Ian. Time was ticking.

I was perusing crappy Hallmark cards at Walgreens when one reached out and struck my brain like a holy bolt of lightning. The front picture was of a girl holding a guitar and singing with little hearts coming out of her mouth.

Boom!

I will write him a love song!

I grabbed a glitter gel pen and a notebook, and I was well on my way to wifey greatness when Ian called.

"Hey, hon," he said. "I'm running a little late, okay? Can we do anniversary stuff at five?"

"Works for me!" I said, all casual-like, as if he didn't just gift me the extra time I needed to write our anniversary ballad. "See you then."

I dusted off the guitar that I bought in high school, tuned it, and got straight to work.

LOVE SONG TO IAN

How can I tell you the ways I feel loved
It's hard to explain, like a gift from above
I'm so thankful to God for the person you are
It's like you were made for my heart

Like you knooooooow me
Heart and souuuuuul me

The reeeeeeeeal me
The way you feeeeeel me

How can I tell you
The way that I love you
all of you
For how you

Love meeeeee.

Wow, this is so good, I thought to myself. *He's going to be blown away.* It did not occur to me that a love song about somebody else should not have the word *me* in it so much. And maybe that's a commentary that Ian would have offered, had he ever gotten a chance to hear it. Too bad the train would never make it to that station.

I packed up my guitar, folded up the lyrics, and headed to our basement apartment for some romantic anniversary memory making.

I arrived at five o'clock on the dot, and Ian was waiting at the door with a smile.

"You have to close your eyes, okay?" he said.

"Should I get all of my things out of the car first?" I responded.

"No, no. All of that can wait." He smiled. His blue eyes sparkled. "Just close your eyes and take my hands."

And so I did.

He led me into the house and down the stairs.

"Careful," he said. "One last step!"

I knew our twenty-two-square-foot apartment like the back

of my hand, but I pretended to need his guidance. I mean, it was sweet. This was the kind of stuff Matthew McConaughey movies were made of. Past the bathroom, to our bedside. He asked me to sit.

"But don't open your eyes, okay! Not yet!"

All of a sudden I started to wonder if Doris was right. I was hoping a coupon wasn't immediately involved in this exchange. My hair still smelled like barbecue, and nothing is less sexy than a walking pork sandwich.

Ian interrupted my thoughts.

"Are you ready? Aaaaaand....*Open!*"

I opened my eyes, and right in front of me was our chest of drawers. Above it, a large mirror. And in front of the mirror...a plastic box. It was over a foot tall and about three feet long, and I realized that my lamp and jewelry bowl were gone and in their place was...

A rat cage.

"His name is Mr. Jingles!" Ian said. He was referencing the mouse character in my favorite movie, but this was no freaking mouse. No, no. This was a Teenage Mutant Ninja Turtles Master Splinter–level rat. Gray fur, pink fleshy tail, and—help me, Jesus—very large testicles.

I sat there, dumbfounded, as my husband continued to yammer on about how this new addition to our family was going to bring joy or something. It's hard to recall, because his voice droned in and out like the teacher in a Charlie Brown special.

All I remember is Ian was going on about how clean rats are, and matchboxes and beans, and it was in that moment that

Mr. Jingles bent his head down over his stomach and began to chew on his balls.

"Out," I said.

"Wait...what?" Ian asked.

"Out. Get it out. Get it...You know what? *You get out.* You and the rat. Out. *Now!*"

"Babe!" Ian seemed genuinely distraught. "Ed's Pet World doesn't give refunds. They'll probably feed him to a snake or something. Can you just *think* about this?"

My head spun around three times, and I am pretty sure bees flew out of my mouth. I simply yelled *"Out!"* until my husband and Mr. Jingles were gone, and then I fell back on the bed, crying.

My sister lived two levels above our basement apartment, and I guess bees travel quickly, because I immediately got a text asking if I was okay. Which, no. I was not. Not even a little.

Karen Leigh, my sister, watched from the upstairs window until Ian left. She saw him put a rat cage in the back seat of his car, and she quickly put two and two together. She came downstairs to comfort me but was having a very hard time keeping a straight face.

"It's not funny, Sis," I sobbed. "Our marriage is over. He gave me a rat for our very first anniversary. A *rat*!"

"Your marriage isn't over," she said, rubbing my back. "But y'all do have some work to do."

"Sis. It had balls. My anniversary present chewed on its own rat *balls*."

"Look, I agree...this is bad. Rats make terrible anniversary presents. But let me ask you this: Did Ian mean to hurt your feelings?"

"No."

"Okay, and does he care that he hurt you?"

"I dunno. Maybe. He took the rat with him."

"Well, if he didn't mean to hurt you, and he cares that you are upset, then your marriage will probably survive this."

Sis rubbed my back and let me cry into my pillow until we heard the sound of Ian's car pulling into the driveway. Then she disappeared upstairs and left me alone to face my dissolving union.

Ian walked into the apartment silently. I could feel him staring and twiddling his fingers, unsure how to proceed. But I couldn't smell a rat, so that was good. I sat up in the bed, my face red and swollen.

"Did they take Mr. Jingles back?"

"They did."

"Are they gonna feed him to a snake?"

"No, and they gave me a seventy-five-dollar gift card for the cage and food and stuff."

"Seventy-five dollars is a lot of money."

"Yeah…you're right. It is."

I could hear a creak inside my soul. It felt like a dam was about to explode. This break was a long time coming.

"What were we thinking, Ian? Our wedding was a mess. Our honeymoon was a mess. Our anniversary is ruined. Let's just face it: This whole marriage is a disaster! We don't even have seventy-five dollars for groceries, Ian. What are we gonna eat from Ed's Pet World?"

He sat there in silence. Not one word. It was time for me to draw the line.

"Ian, you have two choices. We either go back to Mark and Cynthia, or we are getting a divorce!"

Now was the moment for my husband to choose to either cower away from our problems or stand up and fight like a man.

What he did was neither of those things.

Ian sat down on the bed, put his hand against his forehead, and started laughing.

I waited for a second. I remember Momma doing this once. Maybe I broke Ian, too. I'd give him time. He needed a moment. Clearly.

A moment passed. He was still laughing. I could feel my blood pressure rise.

"Ian...what the hell is so funny?"

"I'm sorry. It's not. It's just...Mark and Cynthia? Our pre-marital counselors?"

"Yeah?"

"They got a divorce."

"Oh," I replied.

Well, I hadn't seen that coming.

Ian lay back on the bed. Side by side, we both stared at the ceiling fan.

"So," he said. "Is there a third option? An option C? Cause I really don't want a divorce."

I couldn't help it. I laughed. The whole thing was absurd. It was rage inducing and hilarious. I was tickled and furious. I was in love with my husband but also, in that moment, very much over him. None of it made any sense, but Ian was still my best friend. I wasn't in the mood for fighting anymore, least of all with him. A third option did sound good.

Option C turned out to be grace.

I had to forgive Ian for the anniversary rat. To be fair, he'd forgiven me for swearing off baby-making the very first day of our honeymoon. That wasn't my best moment. And this wasn't his.

I told you we married young, dumb, and poor, right?

Ian and I had a lot of growing up to do then, and fifteen years later, we still do. It's easy for me to tell stories about Mr. Jingles making a snack of his nuggets when my husband is the butt of the joke. But the truth of the matter is, in that phase of life, I was just as selfish and even more ridiculous.

For our anniversary last year, I pulled out a shoebox that contained some of my favorite memories from the early years of our relationship. I laughed at the poetry and the faded photographs. I held a few playbills of Broadway shows we had seen over the years. And then I found it: a weathered envelope. ONE YEAR ANNIVERSARY was scrawled across the front. In it were the folded-up lyrics to a horrible love song and a seventy-five-dollar gift card to Ed's Pet World. A reminder of early lessons in grace and forgiveness.

I believe Ms. Doris would have been proud. It was a year of paper, indeed.

· · · · · · · ·

One of the weirdest romantic movie scenes takes place in the film *The Notebook*. The smitten couple are visiting a beach when Allie starts chasing seagulls. As they fly away, she beams at her lover and asks a nonsensical question. Does he think she could have been a bird in another life? He balks a bit, so she argues her case by twirling around in the sand and flapping her arms. Noah smiles and draws her near. "You're a bird," he whispers. But Allie needs Noah to take one more step. He must join her in birdy bliss. Noah responds with the infamous line that ruined a thousand relationships. Setting a bar so high, so covered in sap, that no mortal man could clear it.

"If you're a bird, I'm a bird."

Sigh. I just can't, y'all.

Some of our biggest messes are born in the collision of reality and expectation.

Don't get me started on where these expectations come from. We can't all blame Nicholas Sparks. The secular world can surely send twisted-up messages, but so do people of faith. In our effort to encourage a family unit, we place a very high premium on marriage. So much so, that growing up, every girl in youth group desperately prayed for her husband. And listen…praying is great. But this wasn't like "keep this man safe." It was like begging God to come through in the clutch and send Prince Charming to complete us.

Guess what a husband is not gonna do? Make you feel complete. He's not gonna sweep you up out of your life and take you to chase seagulls on the beach. And if he does, your hair will definitely get frizzy, and I've got news for you: Birds poop a lot. And "you're a bird, I'm a bird"? Maybe this month. But in life, people evolve. You won't always be perfectly cohesive. And if you're expecting Noah to show up to your anniversary with flowers and swoon-worthy monologue—what happens when it's simply the man that you married, smiling and holding a rat?

Rats are gonna happen, people. They just are. Probably not literally, like poor Mr. Jingles. But still.

And the only way you will survive that mess is if you remove the bars someone else set. Notice that I didn't say to lower the bar. I'm just saying *know who set it*. There are some ideals that no human can meet. And those expectations only cause trouble. Sure, Noah is perfect in that romantic movie. But we only saw their highlight reel. If they were real people, and we saw their whole story, what moments would we see unfold? Would they fight every Christmas about which set of grandparents to visit with all of the kids? Would he have dragon breath after drinking coffee? Would she run up the credit cards shopping?

It seems important to remind you that God doesn't go around creating half-made human beings. You are a whole entire person with your very own ideas, dreams, and purpose in life. The only thing you need to be complete is grace, and that comes from God, who *is* perfect. And this should be good news! The pressure is off for us to fulfill or fix one another. That was never the purpose of love. The strongest relationships hold space for the messes and can offer grace for each other's imperfections. They have good times and bad, roses and rats. And in every season, they cling to one another, holy hot mess and all.

> The strongest relationships hold space for the messes and can offer grace for each other's imperfections.

CHAPTER 11

BAGGAGE CLAIM

You've got to always go back in time if you want to
move forward.

—Snoop Dogg

I love going to the airport. It's one of my favorite places in the
world. Airports are like strange little islands where societal
rules disappear.

Pizza and beer for breakfast? Go for it. Sweatpants with sti-
lettos? Why not. Wanna buy trash novels at Hudson Booksell-
ers and drink vodka all alone until your name is called on the
overhead speaker because you're about to miss your flight? I'm
concerned, but there are no rules against it.

In fact, the only hard rules in airports exist to keep travelers
moving along. Take your shoes off in security. Keep your eye

on your own baggage. Leave your emotional support peacock at home. That sort of thing. As long as you aren't holding up travel, that Bloody Mary is nobody's concern.

But there are some lesser-known rules of air travel. Some secret social contracts. Things like: Don't order a fish burrito to eat on the flight. Don't take up both armrests. Don't recline your seat if someone is behind you. Don't clip your toenails midflight.

While airport rules keep travelers moving, these are the rules that keep travelers happy. I mean, no, an ahi taco won't get you kicked off a plane, but it might make your aisle mate dry heave. I know you don't want that, and I don't either, so we suck it up and eat sandwiches instead.

We all agree to these unspoken rules because they make life more pleasant for everyone. And if we are stuck on this journey together, we might as well not be miserable, right?

I think this is why I love airports, y'all. (Well, this and all the people-watching opportunities.) There's a hive behavior, a community vibe that is generally kind and purposeful. If there are two security lines feeding to one TSA agent, the hive files into a pattern. If a sweet little old lady is struggling with the overhead bin, there's a person from the community ready to help her.

"Here you go, ma'am," they will say with a smile, lifting her bag overhead. Then they'll step out of the way so she can get to her seat. And we will all smile and shuffle on by, tucking our elbows in.

Adults wave at babies. Toddlers get airplane pins. The plane goes bump midflight, and everyone laughs nervously. Whether it's kindness or common purpose that creates this solidarity, it doesn't matter. It's special and I adore it. From ticketing to take-off, people are so decent. The journey brings us together.

But holy smokes, when that plane lands, Jesus has left the building. I don't know what happens—is everyone just tired? Under- or over-caffeinated? Perhaps it's that weird recirculated air that everyone has been breathing. I'll give folks credit for being a little stir crazy (those seats are like two inches wide, after all). But between the full day of travel and that stampede off the plane, something happens to those lovely people who just hours ago were smiling and waving at babies. Their social contracts have died. All community is out the window. They arrive at the baggage claim ready to rumble.

Welcome to the Thunderdome.

• • • • • • •

It's 2012, and I'm working as a waitress at a greasy spoon diner called Junior's. My shift ends after breakfast, so I head back home with an apron full of cash. Walking through the front door, I yawn loudly and dump my apron into "The Bowl."

The Bowl is my family's version of a junk drawer. It is a ginormous catch-all that sits on the kitchen counter containing mail, keys, gum, and a whole bunch of stuff we should probably throw away but don't, for God-knows-what-reason.

I notice something new is sitting in The Bowl. It's an envelope—but not of the basic variety. This isn't a bill or a credit card offer. This puppy cost some serious money to produce. It is dark maroon, with shimmering gold embossments. For a moment I wonder who is getting married, and why on earth they chose maroon and gold as wedding colors. Then, in slow motion, it hits me: These are my high school colors. And…it's 2012. That's ten years since my high school graduation. I know what this envelope holds!

How did they find me? I thought to myself, as if I have been in witness protection or something.

"Are you gonna go?" Ian asked.

"No," I said, crumpling the envelope and tossing it toward the trash.

"You missed," he replied with a sip of his coffee. He walked away quietly laughing.

I wanted to throw a rock at his head.

Ian was laughing because a few years prior, I'd received a similar invitation from my high school cheerleading squad. Some of the girls were planning a reunion, and since I was the captain (don't ask; I don't know) they hoped that I would help.

The event was enthusiastically dubbed a "cheerunion," and I was looking forward to it as much as a Pap smear. So, what did my co-dependent, not-yet-going-to-therapy, twenty-something self do? Y'all. Not only did I agree to the flippin' cheerunion, I offered to host the dang thing at my family's lake house.

Go go Gadget: panic attack!

The week leading up to that three-night slumber party, I lost six pounds due to IBS. I needed to get out of this nightmare scenario, if only for the sake of my bowels. So, I tried my darndest to concoct a story, some freakish scenario, that could win me a canceled reunion. It had to be unexpected and crazy, but also somewhat believable.

"How about I got bit by a possum while taking out the trash, and I'm under a three-day rabies observation at the hospital?" I asked Ian, assuming he would find this reasonable.

"No."

"Why?"

"One, that is a terrible lie. And two, possums don't get rabies."

"Okay…so, what if my car is towed because I forgot to pay my parking tickets, and I don't have enough money to bail it out of car jail? People will believe that! Everyone will believe that!"

"You can borrow my car," Ian responded.

"You need your car," I argued.

"MK." Ian gave me a hug. "I love you. But pack your bags."

I arrived at the lake before anyone else and spent some time sweeping up dust bunnies. When the house looked decent, I went to the bathroom to freshen up my face. I straightened my hair, then put it in a ponytail, then brushed it and straightened it again. Looking in the mirror I was suddenly aware of how much time had passed since high school.

Am I really eight years older than I was eight years ago? Okay, obviously. But…eight years? Wasn't high school just last week? If eight years feels like a single week, then in three months I'll be eighty. Is that a wrinkle on my forehead? I'm not ready to die!

That's when I heard the first car pull up, followed immediately by a second and third. Of course everyone was going to arrive in the middle of my existential crisis. Doors were closing and women were squealing; I could hear them through multiple walls. The cheerunion had officially begun. I could feel my heartbeat in my ears.

I splashed water on my face and pulled my hair up again. I needed to get it together. The ponytail made me look younger, I decided. Closer to eighteen than eighty. I took a deep breath and headed outside to welcome all of my guests.

Women who, just eight years prior, made high school a living hell.

• • • • • • •

I'm pretty sure the baggage claim is Dante's seventh circle. If you reject Jesus and support Alabama football, that's where you go when you die. The goal is to get out of this place as quickly as possible, without any human interaction. No casual talk, no people watching, no eye contact. Just focus on the task at hand, and you'll make it out alive. Collect your luggage, and you get to leave. It's your ticket out of the hellscape.

If you want to see humanity at its worst, try the baggage claim at midnight. That sweet man who helped granny with the overhead bin? Yeah, he just knocked her over, walker and all, when the carousel started beeping. That neighborly woman who cooed at your baby as she walked down the aisle? She hissed like a cat when you accidentally reached for her suitcase. Purple flowers, not dots! (How dare you!)

These people were lovely just hours ago. They were part of your traveling community. There was goodness in their actions, their smiles, and their eyes. *What in the cornbread hell happened?* Did somebody spike their Bloody Mary with mean juice? Did they slip in the bathroom and land in toxic sludge?

What makes good people turn into such monsters?

• • • • • • •

After several hours of high-energy chatter and snacking around the kitchen, the girls found their bedrooms, unpacked their bags, and went about their bedtime routines. After washing faces, putting on jammies, and calling to check on our families, we trickled into the family room and curled up like cats on the furniture. Under our blankets, with glasses of wine, the discussions grew more serious. Conversations circled around memories, and classmates we had lost. The girls talked about things they wished they'd done differently and moments they'd have loved to relive. I stayed on the outskirts of those conversations, quietly sipping my wine. I did my best to avoid eye contact, but I could feel something rising within me. Maybe it was heat from a bold merlot, or anger from hurt in my past. Who knows? But I found myself squirming around in my seat, feeling an itch in my soul. People pleasers try to maintain peace, even at the expense of their own. I didn't want a confrontation. The idea of one made me sick. But the truth teller in me knew if they asked, I would be honest about my pain. I would be mad. I would probably cry. I would definitely ruin the party.

"So, MK..." Cara smiled from her perch on the couch. "What have you missed the most about high school?"

Crap.

"OMG, yes—you tell us, MK. You're the host. It's your turn to share!"

"Well, I was pretty miserable in high school. Honestly, I haven't missed anything."

There was a moment of quiet, which I had expected. I'd

broken the number one high school reunion rule. Well, maybe number two. Don't get sloppy and make out with ex-boyfriends would probably be number one. But a close second is trashing the golden days.

Well, I'd already gone this far.

"Okay, I have to be honest," I said, setting my wine down on a side table. "Today has been so much fun. It's weird, because we have so much in common now that I…it's like I really believe we were friends."

I could tell the protests were coming, so I took a deep breath and kept going.

"I know this seems silly, because it's been so long, but I'm still hurt about how y'all treated me. When I was voted captain, it felt like the biggest honor. But then y'all went behind my back to the coach with a petition to remove me from the position. Do you have any idea how that made me feel? To see all of my friends' signatures on that paper? I felt betrayed. Hated. Humiliated. And none of y'all ever apologized."

At this point I was practically sobbing, and the room was full of stunned faces. I wiped my tears with the back of my hand and swallowed the last bit of wine.

I am gonna kill Ian for making me come to this. The possum story was totally believable, I thought.

"MK," Sara spoke up first. "I am sorry. I had no idea you felt so hurt. We all sort of figured you saw that coming, since you skipped cheer camp, and all."

A few of the girls shook their head in agreement, adjusting their blankets uncomfortably.

"You thought I just *skipped* camp?" I asked. "Like I didn't... *want* to go?"

"Uh, yes?" Sara responded, confused. "You never told us otherwise."

"I just..." I stopped to steady myself. "I assumed everyone knew."

This was like a nightmare coming to life. I caught the face of my closest friend. She nodded her head and encouraged me to go on.

"I was at grand jury for my child abuse case. To testify against my former stepfather. It was three days of recorded forensic testimony. One of the worst weeks of my life. He had abused me since the second grade. Mom didn't know, obviously. Dad couldn't have known it, either. But it ripped my world apart, and the week of cheer camp, I was being cross-examined by lawyers. That's why our coach refused the petition. And it's also why I spent the rest of high school assuming everyone hated me. I really thought y'all knew..."

"Oh my God, Mary Katherine," Sara said. And for a moment, that's all there was.

And then, something happened, that to this day breaks me in the best possible way. One by one, the women got up and walked over to my chair.

They huddled around me, wrapped me in love, and together, we cried healing tears.

• • • • • •

Looking back, that cheerunion was like a baggage claim session at the end of a very long flight. I was heaving my suitcase of family trauma, and they had their fully packed duffels, too. I didn't know what was in their bags or what they had assumed about me. And they didn't know what was in my luggage, or that I was seriously in need of support.

In high school, we all had just jostled against each other, confused and in pain, none of us seeing the others. I left after graduation, believing they were just a pack of pom-pom-carrying biddies. And they thought I was an apathetic no-show to an important event for our squad. Only eight years later, we were mature enough to see what we'd all been carrying around. And finally, finally start the process of unpacking all that hurt.

Now, I'm not saying that every social interaction should end with baggage being dumped on the floor. There's a time when it's appropriate to unload your luggage, and a time when you should roll it along. We've all had to wiggle nervously in our seats at a dinner party that takes a hard left turn. When some boozy guest decides to unpack and nobody knows how to respond. It's like a suitcase tumbling down the ramp and busting open in front of the crowd. Circling the carousel with a week's worth of dirty underwear on display. I've been that person, and I've seen that person, and my goodness. It's just not necessary.

There are rules at the baggage claim that, if followed, can prevent this kind of thing from happening. I personally think they should be printed in red ink and repeated over every airport loudspeaker in the world. They are as follows:

1. Don't crowd the carousel.
2. Step away to get situated.
3. Mark your suitcase.
4. Don't be a jerk.

Okay, that's the posterboard version. But now, let's sit down and have a fireside chat. I imagine you know where I'm going. Folks, our life is nothing if not a constant journey. We are travelers together in this airport. Sometimes we don't have a destination fully planned, but we are moving along just the same. And I think, for the most part, we are doing our best to be decent to one another. Because we might as well not be miserable, right? But there are days when your fellow travelers are tired, or drunk, or their plans have been inevitably delayed. Maybe they just lost a loved one, or a job. Maybe they are sick of airplane sandwiches. Who knows?

You don't. And that's the whole point.

We are all just here, trying to manage our own freaking baggage, when occasionally things go sideways. The man on that flight who helped the granny with her suitcase was the same man who knocked her over. The lady who waved at your baby was the same lady who hissed when you reached for her suitcase. People are people; we aren't all good or all bad. We're all trying to be on our best behavior, but sometimes we mess up. One glass of merlot, and the next thing we know, some trauma comes busting through the zipper. But it doesn't have to be that way. Let's revisit the ways we reclaim our baggage and figure out how to do it with grace, okay?

Don't Crowd the Carousel: Wisdom would have us avoid any place where you see everyone around you leaving with baggage. In an airport, that's not possible, but in life, it certainly is. Use discretion about where you invest your time, energy, and attention. If your circle of influence is toxic and hurtful, you should leave before you are hurt, too. Who needs another bag to carry? <looks around> I don't.

Step Away to Get Situated: Nobody wants to be up in your space while you're handling your baggage situation. When you are wrestling with things that make you angry, do that in therapy, with a loved one, or with a minister. Don't let your baggage bang into other people because you refused to deal with it properly.

Mark Your Suitcase: We're all grown-ups, right? We should be able to identify our own baggage. By knowing what your own struggles are and what they look like, you are less likely to cause chaos and hurt someone you love. Slap a sparkly unicorn luggage tag on those daddy issues. Work through them in therapy, not with your spouse. Tie a yellow ribbon on those body confidence struggles to help you keep an eye out for them. You don't want your daughter repeating the words you attack yourself with in the mirror. And while we're talking about marking our own luggage so we don't unintentionally hand it off to those nearest and dearest, we've all got to make sure that we're only carrying *our* *own* baggage, and not everyone else's. (Are you listening, my people-pleasing friends? This especially applies to you.)

Don't Be a Jerk: All those people hustling through life? They don't know what's in your head. And despite the fact it would make life easier, you don't know what's in theirs. We are all trying to get to wherever we're going without losing our socks on the floor.

Trust me, I know this process is exhausting, but it's necessary for your spiritual growth. There have been times in my life when my circumstances looked like a cluster of baggage. A mess so overwhelming, so heavy with shame, that I was certain I would disappear beneath it all.

The thing is, so often we buy into this narrative that we must reinvent who we are in order to grow. As if a new set of behaviors or some new age idea is enough to bid baggage goodbye. I see this mindset play out every January, when millions of people declare "New Year, new me!" I get caught up in this, too. Then two weeks later, when the diet is broken, or the budget fails, or the fancy new planner remains empty—I feel even more depressed and defeated. The reality is that it's "New year, same me." It's how you navigate each new season that makes the biggest difference.

We don't need to re-create ourselves. God did just fine in

> The reality is that it's "New year, same me." It's how you navigate each new season.

that department. We just need to open up the suitcase we are carrying and figure out where everything is stuffed. We need to study the things that weigh heavy on our hearts. Understand our hurt and where it comes from.

It's a scary thing, standing at that carousel. What's coming around is bound to be heavy. But when you stare down your insecurities and traumas, that's when you are at your bravest.

The baggage claim is the final stop before you leave the airport. Grab your things and you're well on your way…at least, until the next journey. In the meantime, remember to hold grace for others; everyone is pulling their own luggage. Today it is them; tomorrow it's you. The carousel of life goes round and round.

Or, as Ian Maclaren famously said, "Be kind, for everyone you meet is fighting a hard battle."

A battle at the baggage claim.

> Remember to hold grace for others; everyone is pulling their own luggage. Today it is them; tomorrow it's you.

CHAPTER 12

BIRTH IS
A MESSY AFFAIR

Flesh gives birth to flesh, but the Spirit gives birth to spirit. You should not be surprised at my saying, "You must be born again."

—John 3:6–7

Back when the dinosaurs roamed the earth, I decided to join a sorority. This is a fact I am hesitant to admit, knowing so many folks side-eye the Greeks. To be fair, there are bad apples who headline the news and muck things up for the rest of us, but you know I'm a truth teller, and this is my truth: My time in AOII was wonderful.

I enjoyed getting to know that diverse group of women, and I loved kicking butt at flag football. When we got big sisters, I pretty much struck gold and made a friend who would end up in my wedding.

Lindsey was a pre-med student who had her whole entire life together. She was the yin to my yang, the calm to my crazy. And looking back, that was probably the point. It was Lindsey's responsibility to look after me, and she took that job very seriously. I got wake-up calls for my early morning classes, fussy voicemails if I ever slept in. She cooked cheese grits for dinner when I missed Momma, and she steered me away from frat houses. Lindsey drove me home when I first got drunk, picking burritos up along the way. She advised against my poor life choices, but I mostly ignored her advice. Still, a special bond formed between us, both familial and light. I loosened Lindsey up, and she kept me in line. In that way, we were perfectly matched.

The week before initiation, Lindsey called me up for coffee. When I hopped in the car, her sunglasses were on and the look on her face was stern. She didn't have pandas or glittery cups. No Tupperware containers of grits. Not one for pretense, she handed me a latte and gave me a bit of her mind.

"MK, you are a silly person. You know that I love that about you. But our initiation ceremony is coming up Thursday, and you have to take it seriously. I'm your Big, but I'm also the president. This ritual *matters* to me. It's not just about sharing sisterhood; it's about sharing values, too. This is a commitment, MK. Are you ready to cut out the partying and actually go to class? Can you behave like you represent a group? Because that's what this is about. I'll be your friend whatever you choose. Call me when you get up tomorrow."

And that was the end of our coffee date. I went back to my dorm in a funk.

• • • • • • •

Can I speak candidly? Of course, I can. Birth is a messy affair.

Seriously, the first time I gave birth, I literally pooped on my doctor. She swept it away like no big deal, but I was downright mortified.

"*Ohmygosh*, did I just...?" I yelled from the peak of the stirrups.

She waved her hand dismissively. "Don't worry about it. *PUSH!*"

I wanted to argue, but I couldn't breathe. My body felt like a tube of toothpaste contracting out its contents. I closed my eyes, gritted my teeth, and pushed with all of my might. With a woosh of only the Lord knows what, out came Benjamin Ty. He was purple and covered in cottage cheese and sounded like a sad little kitten. *But!* He passed his Apgar and had all his fingers and toes. I laid my head down and counted my blessings, wondering what in the world just happened.

There are women who talk about childbirth like it's their favorite thing on the planet. Honestly, I am confounded by this. What exactly is the appeal? Perhaps these women had dolphin births. I read an article about that once. People fly to the Caribbean and set up shop in some heavenly beachside cabana. When it's go time, they give birth in crystal blue waters, with Flipper cheering them on. I'm not gonna lie: This scenario intrigued me for a moment, until I vetted it further. I know how this would play out for somebody like me. After flying over the ocean nine months pregnant, I would arrive at my cabana on the beach, which would be sweltering and full of mosquitos. And then there'd be a cabana boy, which would be nice if I could actually drink a piña colada. *I'll have a water, please. And an anesthesiologist. What, no epidurals in a Caribbean hut? Why did I do this again?*

So, in active labor, I would waddle toward the ocean, and almost certainly fall in the sand. I would roll around crying like a sad, sweaty manatee, trying to get back up. I would scream. I would cuss. I would threaten my husband with divorce. But with ten thousand dollars spent on this magical experience, I would refuse to give up at that point. So, to the horror of tourists and locals alike, I would barrel-roll my way to the water. And that, for me, is where the true horror show begins. Assuming my husband hasn't caught the first flight home, what happens when I actually push? Where does that pre-baby woosh go? Wouldn't the waves just…wash it all back? That sounds so…magical and worth my money. What more could a woman want? Oh right, while I'm actively laboring in those wooshy waves, let's add sea creatures to this scenario. Those are definitely dolphin fins circling the water, right? This isn't disconcerting at all.

As a writer on the topic of parenting, I've read birth stories from women around the world. Some who were poor, some who were wealthy. Different countries, cultures, and ethnicities. Can I let you in on a secret? Whether these women were in a hospital bed, or a tub in their living room, or a villa in Siesta Key, they all experienced some level of suffering. Birth is a process that is no less primal than it was at the beginning of time. Even in a room full of doctors and monitors, delivery can be unpredictable. It's a scary, miraculous roller-coaster ride, and at the end of it, of course, there is joy. Celebration for the new beginning of life. Relief for an exhausted mother.

But before the birth and the joyous celebrations, there's a woman who inevitably hurts.

• • • • • • •

The night before initiation, I couldn't sleep. I was ruminating over Lindsey's words. No, not the part about going to class. Not the part about partying less. Not the part about taking life seriously. Y'all, I wish I had been that mature. No, of all of the things Lindsey said to me, what kept me awake was this: "This ritual *matters* to me."

What the heck was a ritual?

I couldn't stop my mind from racing. What the heck had I signed up for? Would there be candles and stone stairs that descended into a creepy, dark basement? I remembered a movie about a secret society. What was it called? *The Skulls?* Yeah, those guys were drugged and put into coffins, so they could be "born again" in their ritual. *Oh gosh*, I thought, jumping up to my laptop. Google: *initiation rituals*. Holy cow, another one. This sorority apparently strips down to their panties and climbs up this weird tunnel during initiation. The whole thing is supposed to represent a womb, so they can be born again as new members.

There was no way in heck I could do any of this. I waited 'til morning to call Lindsey.

One thirty a.m.

Two a.m.

Three a.m.

Three thirty a.m.

Five a.m., thank goodness, good enough.

"Hey, Linds, are you awake? It's important," I texted. A few minutes later, she called.

"MK?" She seemed pretty confused. Which was fair, since she was typically my wake-up call. "Everything okay?"

"Yeah, it's this AOII stuff. I've been thinking about it."

"Okay."

"I can't crawl in a coffin or up some fake uterus for a rebirthing initiation thing. I just need to know about this ritual. I didn't sleep at all last night."

"MK."

"Yes?"

"Are you serious?"

"Yes."

"No coffins or uteruses. Promise."

"Phew," I said, my anxieties quelled. "I guess I'll see you tonight!"

"It's nothing to worry about," Lindsey assured me. "Just bring a squirrel for the animal sacrifice."

• • • • • • •

I admit, when I hear the term "born-again Christian," my nose crinkles up with discomfort. It's a Christianese phrase that gets lost in translation and can invoke a whole mess of imagery. Some might imagine a televangelist type, selling miracles for three easy payments. Others perhaps see an angry fundamentalist, hell-bent on condemning his neighbors. For pragmatists, it brings forth more questions than answers. Which I get; it's a pretty wild analogy.

The first time Jesus discussed rebirth, there was one of *those* guys in the crowd. He was a religious scholar named Nicodemus, and he believed Jesus was crazy.

"Uh, hello," Nic said (to paraphrase). "How can someone be born when they are old? Do you expect them to go back into their mother's womb?"

I imagine the crowd roared with laughter. I wonder if I'd have laughed with them.

But Jesus responded with patience and grace, unfurling the meaning of His words.

> *Flesh gives birth to flesh, but the Spirit gives birth to spirit…"You must be born again."*

In biblical times, there were no birthing centers or Caribbean dolphin deliveries. There were no epidurals or constant monitors, no tests that could mitigate risk. The crowd that was gathered at the temple that day knew nothing of modern medicine. They had never seen a Hollywood movie where the baby came out pink and perfect. Those who were gathered knew labor and suffering—the messiest side of childbirth. And yet Jesus told them, in the plainest of terms, that their spirits must be *reborn*.

As a mother of two, it makes sense to me now, what Jesus was teaching those rabbis. We all have a spirit, asleep in its mess. Buried beneath our baggage. To bring it to life would be a miraculous thing, and that is what Jesus was offering. To be able to experience life and hope in abundance. But before that birth, and the joyous celebration, there's a human who inevitably hurts. Spiritual birth is a messy affair. And mine was no exception.

• • • • • • •

I wish I could tell you that the changes you want to make in your life will be easy. But experience (as well as Scripture) tells me that this kind of journey is hard. An extreme upside, I am pleased to tell you, is there are no squirrel sacrifices involved. There are no candles or long stone stairways. No fake uteruses to bring you forth into the world. The ritual takes place in the depths of your heart. It's as simple as calling upon His name.

I'm not going to lie, there are still some scary moments while walking with Jesus. Sometimes, my faith feels strange and uncomfortable—and I've gone to church my whole life. I once shared my faith with a stranger on a plane, and I thought things were going quite well. Until he rang for an attendant, requested a beer, and said, "My friend here talks to ghosts."

The Gospel tends to make people look crazy. Can I tell y'all about my baptism? I slipped down the stairs and hit the water with all the grace of an orca. Then I popped up like a buoy, grinning ear to ear, my robe clinging to my inner thighs. It was a SeaWorld-worthy spectacle. I couldn't have been more awkward.

Hello, church. I'm Mary Katherine! I'm here to make everything weird!

What I'm saying is, chasing Jesus won't make anyone cool. Faith is a lifelong trudge toward holiness that has humbled the proudest of hearts. But if you want to truly drop your baggage and experience a deep shift from where you've been to where you need to be…it's gonna take a complete spiritual transformation, a ritual change of the heart. A rebirth.

It's gonna take Jesus.

CHAPTER 13

THE MAGIC OF THE MOON

Don't tell me the moon is shining; show me the glint of
light on broken glass.

—Anton Chekhov

I climbed over the middle of Momma's station wagon to the
bench that faced the back window. The air-conditioner never
reached the "back-back," but at five years old, I didn't mind. I
opened my lunch box and pulled out some raisins and a Hi-C
Ecto Cooler.

Mmmmm, that sugary goodness.

Technically, it was against the rules to drink juice in the car,
but Momma didn't seem to care much lately. And besides, I was
the family outlaw, always getting in trouble. My grandmother
said that I needed more spankings, but I think she was wrong: To

me, the punishment was worth the crime. Especially when the crime looked like an ice-cold box of Hi-C Ecto Cooler.

The driver door slammed and Momma sat down, pausing behind the wheel. Then she took a deep breath and adjusted the rearview to get a glimpse of her babies: my toddler brother, secure in his car seat, playing with Matchbox cars. My nine-year-old sister, sniffling loudly and reading the Berenstain Bears. And me, in the back-back with my Teddy Ruxpin, slurping a contraband punch.

Momma sighed, but as predicted, she didn't bother fussing. She just buckled her seat belt and started the car.

"Well, kids...who's excited?" she asked, forcing a smile.

None of us were excited, and none of us answered, so she pressed the FM radio button, and "Love Shack" came blasting through the speakers. As Momma pulled out of the driveway, I pressed my fingers against the glass. I watched as a little brick rancher slowly faded into the distance. In it: my father, my childhood, and everything that was once familiar.

• • • • • • •

One of the greatest joys of being a mother is sharing words with my children. It's incredible to watch them discover this world while, at the same time, learning to describe it. Everything is magical and waiting to be named.

Like, holy crap, *there is a stick with wings and it's fluttering around my head!*

"Mommy—what's dat?"

"That's a butterfly. Butt-er-fly."

And, OMG, those shiny circles of air always disappear when I catch them!

"Mommy—what's dat?"

"Those are bubbles, baby. Buhhhh-bles."

There are days I feel like Darwin exploring a new land, with two tiny understudies beneath my feet.

My kids ask, "What's dat?" and I give it a name.

It's a dog! It's a pony! It's a lollipop!

I am all knowing. I am all powerful. I have all the answers.

• • • • • • •

The moon was rising along Highway 65 as we traveled toward our new home. My sister and brother were already asleep, and I wasn't too far behind. With my head leaned against the window, I lazily traced the outline of the moon with my little finger. I yawned.

"Momma?"

"Yes, baby?"

"Is the moon following us to Dothan?"

"The moon is always up there, baby. It stays put, wherever you go. You'll see it at our new house, like you saw it at our old house."

I was pretty sure the moon was following me in particular, and Momma was missing the point.

"Okay, so when we get to our new house, the moon is going to be there?"

"Yes."

"And the sun?"

"Yes."

"And my toys?"

"Yes."

"And Baby Brother and Karen Leigh, too?"

"Yes."

I sat quietly for a few more miles, staring out the window. The moon was definitely following us to our new house, so that was a good thing. It couldn't be all that bad if the moon was making the trip.

"Momma?" I asked, dozing off. "What about Daddy? Will he be at the new house, too?"

. . . .

One of the hardest things a mother must do is teach the language of pain. To give her child a word for divorce, or cancer, or death. A word that doesn't give life to something beautiful but, rather, sucks life out of something beautiful.

I remember learning one such word that forever altered my universe. Big fat tears streamed down my cheeks as Momma explained divorce. It was a word that told me love was impermanent, and grief could be felt for the living. I was five years old when Momma explained what it meant for a family to break. And all of a sudden, I understood that the moon didn't really chase cars. It was just an unmagical lump, stuck up in the sky, that I could see wherever I was going.

. . . .

Ten years later, I was a high school cheerleader on a bus bouncing down the interstate. It was a four-hour trip from Dothan, Alabama, to Bayou La Batre, but nobody minded the drive. Nothing could set the cheerleaders abuzz quite like an out-of-town football game (although this one would be yet another heartbreaker). The girls were all pom-poms and giggles and gossip. We had hope and spirit to spare—and the fumes from cans of glitter spray probably contributed to the happy atmosphere.

Conversation circled around boys, and before long, an unfortunate game of Truth or Dare fired up. I had been around those girls long enough to know that "dare" was a fool's choice, so I opted for truth. Besides, chances were slim that my life would yield anything juicy.

"All right, MK," one of the girls asked. "How far have you been with a guy?"

The girls leaned in for my answer, curious what their youth-groupie captain would confess. My response was a disappointment, met with boos and a few tossed pom-poms.

"Sorry, girls," I giggled and shrugged. "You said you wanted the truth!"

But the truth was, I hadn't told the whole truth. I hadn't told anyone at all. The secret I had kept since second grade was becoming harder to hold in. I wanted to tell someone, to be free from the hurt, but I wasn't sure who to trust.

I was just a child, sleeping with stuffed animals, when the sexual abuse began. My former stepfather's shadowy form would loom in my bedroom door. I would close my eyes and hope to disappear. My neon dinosaur never left my side.

When the girls asked me how far I'd been, I suddenly felt sick. That queasy knot sat in my stomach for the entire football game. On the bus ride home from Bayou La Batre that night, I stared out the window and cried. The girls chalked it up to my devastated school spirit, but I couldn't have cared any less. I was contemplating the actual truth, and what would happen if I shared it: Who would believe me, who would it hurt, and how it would upend my life.

· · · · · · ·

During my senior year of high school, every Wednesday was current affairs day in history class. A newspaper was thrown in the middle of a laminate table with some plastic scissors. Our task was to choose an article, summarize it, and report it to the class.

I remember racing to the table that Wednesday, flipping to the middle section, and hoping it wasn't too late. A rectangular-shaped cutout confirmed my worst nightmare.

Thirty minutes later, a clueless young lady was sharing her summary with the class. A well-known local man had been arrested for sexually abusing a minor. Details were vague, but the abuse had gone on for years. Extrapolating from details implied in the article, she said, "I think it was their stepfather!" I shrank down in my seat as she added, "Ew, how gross is that?"

Three years after grand jury, the trial had finally hit the docket. It would take place right before graduation. It was both terrible and perfect timing. Terrible because, once again, my darkest secrets were all over the news. Perfect because it would be over before high school ended. In one day, a plea bargain was reached: Guilty in exchange for no prison time. And just like that, my trauma was over.

Except that, really, it wasn't. I went to college with wounds I didn't know existed. I made horrible choices in an effort to medicate those wounds. I sought comfort and distraction in dark places. I failed classes and compromised friendships. There was no excuse, but there was a reason: I was broken, and broken things don't behave as they should.

• • • • • • •

When I first met Brian, he was sitting on the porch of the Pi Kappa Phi house. I knew he wasn't a fraternity guy, because he stood out like a sore thumb. For one thing, he was very sober, and for another, he wasn't hitting on girls. He just lounged in a chair, bright eyed and friendly, making small talk with anyone who would listen.

"Who is that guy?" I asked a friend who had talked with him over an hour.

"Oh," she said. "You mean Brian? He's president of some Christian group. But he's not weird or anything. He's cool."

It was obvious Brian was a pocket full of sunshine, but his presence at the party unnerved me. Maybe it was his beard, or how folks surrounded him, or his kind and gentle demeanor. Brian reminded me of Jesus. And while I came to that party looking for something, I was pretty sure that wasn't it.

The following Friday, I was back for another party at the Pi Kapp house. I stumbled up the front porch steps, primed to make bad decisions. And lo, there was Frat House Jesus.

"Mary Katherine?" he said, with a friendly voice. "Hey! I'm Brian Fulton!"

I couldn't just ignore the man, when he was practically Fred Rogers. And surprisingly, I didn't want to. His kindness had a gravitational pull. I told my friend I'd catch up with her in a bit and walked across the porch.

"Hey, Brian," I said, taking a seat. "Glad to finally meet you."

A few hours later, I realized I had never gone inside for the party. Instead, I stayed on the porch all night, with Brian and others who had joined. We talked about high school football games, and the best food to order at Al's. We exchanged some roommate horror stories; I laughed more than I had in months. Around midnight, some girls walked out of the house, hanging on one another's shoulders. They were all more than a little bit drunk, including the one holding keys.

"Well, it's been fun," Brian said, hopping out of his seat. "Y'all come by the BCM some time. I literally live upstairs."

Chances were slim that I'd go visit the Baptist Campus Ministries, but I was intrigued by how different Brian was. I watched as he jogged down the sidewalk, caught up with the girls, and asked if he could please drive them home.

"But how will you get back?" the driver asked, handing over her keys.

"Oh, I *love* walking," Brian replied. "And really, it's not that far."

• • • • • •

A few months later, my college boyfriend dumped me and moved on with a gorgeous blonde. I responded in the classiest way possible: by drinking cheap vodka, cutting my bangs, and catching a ride to the frat house.

I'll show him what he's missing.

Holy. Hot. Mess. This probably doesn't have to be said, but I didn't accomplish my goal that night. Instead, I embarrassed myself so badly that my sorority put me on probation. I was no longer allowed at any Greek functions. They were worried I'd make *them* look bad. (Quick tip: If you ever get to a point in your life where the Greeks think you are too wild, it's time to pump the brakes, my friend. You are definitely off the rails.)

A few days later, I found myself alone on the couch, curled up in the fetal position. I had come to college for a fresh new start, outrunning the pain of my childhood. But in one short semester, I had proved to myself what I'd suspected was true all along: I was an unfixable human disaster. An embarrassing, unlovable mess.

My phone vibrated with an incoming text, and I peeled myself off of the couch.

"Hey MK! It's Brian. The BCM has worship at 7. I'd love for you to come."

It was literally the last thing I wanted to do, and I had plenty of reasons to decline. First, it was already 6:45, and my face was swollen from tears. Second, there was thunder rolling in the distance; a storm would pass through soon. But the thoughts in my head were getting dark, and I didn't want to be alone. So I washed my face, threw on a sweatshirt, and fired off a response. Then I tucked my phone in the pocket of my jeans and headed to the BCM.

Brian was in the lobby when I arrived. He gave me a friendly hug.

"I'm so glad you could make it!" he said. "Let me introduce you to some folks."

By the time I took my seat for worship, I'd met half of the BCM. Brian took his place at the front of the room and opened the night with prayer.

I had never heard anyone pray like that. The way he talked to God was so familiar, like he was on the phone with a friend. He spoke so casually, with so much confidence, like he *knew* the Lord was listening. Brian thanked God for being a loving Dad. I had never heard someone call God "Dad" before. What *was* clear to me is that the God Brian loved clearly loved him back.

As Brian offered up his prayer, his face full of joy, a strange feeling crept in my heart. I couldn't discern what it was: A tug? A nudge? A whisper?

Brian opened the floor for prayers, and suddenly my palms were sweaty. I wanted to talk to this "Dad" of his, but I was scared to do it out loud. Which was weird, considering I was raised in church. I'd been praying for most of my life. But the God I knew was always mad or disappointed. I prayed when I needed to say sorry. This was something different. Something I wanted to try. My mouth moved before I gave it permission.

"Um…God?" I mumbled a bit with my words, but the room was respectfully quiet. "Hey, it's me…MK. I mean, obviously You know that. You are God."

My face felt hot and my heart was racing, but I knew I needed to finish. Whatever was happening inside of my heart would probably not follow me home.

"It's been a pretty bad year, God. And I'm feeling...I feel so sad."

My voice cracked when I said *sad*, and I knew my levees were failing.

"I'm sad, and I've been trying to feel better. But everything I do makes it worse. I feel stuck and angry and hurt. And I am tired, God. Please help me. Amen."

The rest of the room said amen, and someone patted my back. When I looked up, Brian was gone and a band had taken the stage. The guitarist had just opened a song when a loud clap of thunder shook the room. Every light in the building went out, and rain started beating the roof.

"Don't worry, everyone," said a familiar voice, with a hint of laughter in his words. It was Brian. "It's only darkness. God isn't gone. Your eyes will adjust soon enough."

The guitarist unplugged his instrument and sat down at the foot of the stage. He picked up the intro where he left off, and soon the whole room joined in.

*Amazing grace, how sweet the sound, that saved a wretch
   like me.
I once was lost but now I'm found, was blind but now
   I see.*

The song seemed to fill the room, our words floating up to the ceiling. Was God in there? Was He listening? I wanted to talk to *Dad*. Not the God that frowned whenever I cussed, but the God who filled faces with joy.

The rain came down even harder.

> *'Twas grace that taught my heart to fear, and grace my fears relieved.*
> *How precious did that grace appear, the hour I first believed.*

My eyes did adjust, and I searched the room, desperate to locate Brian. I realized he'd invited me here for a reason. That he knew something I hadn't known. He knew I was lost, floating around, like a balloon whose string was cut.

• • • • • • •

There's something available to you and me, we who journey through messes in life. We have access to an authentic innocence through God, a restoration of trust. No matter what we've seen or what we've experienced, there is peace when we come to our Father. We can be childlike before Him, asking our questions, letting Him heal and hold us. It's okay to not have all the answers. It's okay to not understand everything. It's okay to admit we are tired of drifting and we long for some hope to ground us.

I'd put trust in people who broke my faith, and that baggage framed how I viewed God. Between my parents' divorce and my former stepfather's abuse, I'd lost my faith in fathers. I tried to imagine a "heavenly Dad" that wouldn't hurt or disappointment me. But everywhere I looked, I saw the potential for hurt and pain and abandonment.

The gospel sounded fresh and exciting to me, like a salve to a lifelong injury. And even though I'd heard that message before, it hit me differently now.

When the storm passed, the lights came on, and the students closed in prayer.

"Hey, Brian," I said. "I have a few questions. Do you mind going for a walk?"

It turned out Brian had told the truth. He really did *love* walking. We walked to my dorm, but that didn't take long, so we circled around the campus. I still had questions, and he still had energy, so we walked a little bit more.

I told him about this hole in my heart, that I never felt I could fill. How childhood had left me a broken person, and college was making it worse.

"Where was God in all of this mess?" I asked. "He just left us here to suffer?"

Brian explained that pain entered the world when we broke our covenant with God. That by choosing sin, we were separated from the One who loves us most.

"A God-shaped hole is the kind of injury nothing on earth can fill. It's why we feel so hollow and sad, when chasing worldly things. But God doesn't relish our suffering. That's why He gave us Christ. To reconcile us back to Him, so we can feel whole again. The world is still a broken place, and suffering won't disappear. But God never leaves you, Mary Katherine. He's with you wherever you go."

This all sounded wild and strange, but I knew in my heart it was true. There was a presence I'd felt in the depths of my soul, otherworldly and familiar. I had more information than I could possibly process, and a million more questions to ask. But I was tired, and my mind was spinning, and I didn't know what else to say. Thankfully, Brian was the type of person who was comfortable walking in silence.

When I got to my dorm, I sat on the couch, where earlier I felt the world crumble. I was still a little sad, which made sense. Sad things had still happened. But something was changing in my spirit. I could feel it happening in real time. It was something that rushed into broken places and filled my heart with hope. It was the voice of a Father, dare I say *Dad*, comforting His daughter. Promising that, no matter what, He'd never leave her side.

Before I fell asleep that night, I opened my bedroom curtains. Hanging high above the campus: a shining, silver moon.

For a while, I stared at my old friend and felt a childlike wonder. It was a feeling I knew from long before, staring through a station wagon window. I could imagine my Heavenly Father up there, shining in all of His glory. Following me around from place to place, for the entire journey of life. I could feel a spark ignite in my soul, and I knew: *I finally believe*. It was a childlike faith, a new understanding of the magic of the moon.

"God never leaves you, Mary Katherine. He's with you wherever you go."

> "God never leaves you, Mary Katherine. He's with you wherever you go."

CHAPTER 14

GUARDRAILS AND POOL NOODLES

Don't ever take a fence down until you know why it was put up.

—Robert Frost

had my first panic attack when I was ten years old. There was no particular reason; it was just the strangest thing. I was lying in bed, minding my own business, when this weird question popped into my brain. It was a strange whisper, both foreign and familiar, like it came from me, but it didn't.

And it said this:

What if my body forgets how to swallow? Will I choke on my spit and die?

The thought of my esophagus closing up shop was something I had never considered. So, to comfort my nerves, I closed my eyes and swallowed a little saliva. Then, I tried it again. And again, and again. And one last time for good measure.

Then, wouldn't you know, with a mouth as dry as cotton, I was suddenly unable to swallow. I jumped out of bed, grasping my throat, and ran to the hallway bathroom. With the water on high, I drank straight from the spicket, soaking my hair and pajamas. I remember sitting on the cold tile floor, wrapped in a towel, unsure if my mind was playing tricks on me or if my body was slowly dying. Those were the only two options, clearly. Neither option was particularly great. I huddled next to that sink for almost an hour, waiting for my throat to stop working. Slowly, my panic subsided, and the impending sense of doom disappeared. I got off the wet floor, went back to my room, and changed into dry pajamas. Under the covers, I closed my eyes again, hoping for a bit of reprieve. And that's when the strange whisper returned once more.

What if I forget how to breathe?

• • • • • • •

One of my favorite characters in the universe of fiction was written by J.R.R. Tolkien. It's not Frodo, or the beloved Samwise Gamgee. No, sir. My weirdo heart belongs to the reviled and wretched creature called Gollum. I admit, he's not immediately lovable. When you first meet him in the books, he's practically a monster, skittering about in the darkness like some giant, hairless squirrel. He survives by eating raw fish and the flesh of goblins. And if that isn't horrible enough, there's a swallowing noise which gurgles in his throat. Hence the name:

Gollum! Gollum!

But, spoiler alert (even though the book is seventy years old): Gollum wasn't always this way. He was once a hobbit by the name of Sméagol, who lived in a peaceful village. On his birthday, he went on a fateful adventure, fishing with his cousin, Deágol. There, his cousin found a gold ring while trying to reel in a large fish. It was in that precise moment when Sméagol's trouble began. Almost immediately, he was affected by the power of the One Ring, and demanded it as a birthday present. When Deágol refused, Sméagol flew into a rage, choking his cousin to death. Exiled from the Riverfolk, Sméagol fled to the mountains, burrowing a home in its caverns. The magic of the One Ring prolonged his life—keeping him alive, but not well. He spent centuries living inside those caves, his spirit and mind deteriorating. His eyes transformed into large orbs. His skin grew gray and pallid. And as he suffered greatly, Gollum refused to venture out in society. He was too paranoid someone might take his true love. The source of his pain.

His Precious.

• • • • • • •

Years into therapy, I finally uncovered the nature of those strange whispers. Those uninvited and disturbing ideas that materialize out of nowhere are called "intrusive thoughts." While not entirely normal for a ten-year-old child, they are a common occurrence in adults. Seriously, ask any mother who has carried her newborn up a flight of stairs. She will tell you there was a moment when her brain betrayed her, and she pictured her child tumbling down. And while she probably questioned her sanity in that moment, her behavior shifted. She gripped her baby closer to her body. Slowed down the pace of her steps. She instinctively exercised more caution as a result of that strange whisper.

Scientists theorize that the purpose of intrusive thoughts is to save us from worst-case scenarios. God created us to protect our species, to predict the things that threaten us. Strange whispers are a prediction system. They tell us we shouldn't walk near the road or a car could run over us. They tell us to move the knife up higher lest, God forbid, tiny fingers could reach. The purpose of those whispers is to give fear within reason. But sometimes, they can go haywire.

When Benjamin was born, I experienced a love that was so all-encompassing it scared the crap out of me. So when those intrusive thoughts inevitably made their way in, I was more fragile than ever before. Whispers of my son choking, or falling and bleeding, turned my whole life upside down.

I went full-on Gollum with postpartum anxiety—a bona fide crazy cave creature. For days at a time, I would stay indoors, just to make sure Ben stayed alive. In my house, no cars drove up on sidewalks. No off-leash dogs could attack. We were fine, except when I had to venture outside for the groceries or church or, you know, life. It was then the whispers would turn into screams:

Are you crazy? It's dangerous out here! Something, anything, could kill you!

Fear has a way of warping the mind, and over time, my isolation grew worse. I truly believed I was the only one who could feed my son a bottle. If someone else tried, they could screw up the formula, and Ben could die from water poisoning. I was the only one who could put my son to bed. Other people might try, but would they check his breathing? Check his hand to make sure it was warm?

Things got harder when Ben started to crawl—as moving children are harder to manage. So, I bought approximately eight thousand pool noodles and a few rolls of duct tape and covered every corner in the house. To be honest, our living room looked like an asylum, which I guess was exactly the point. I had mitigated every possible risk. There was no hint of danger. No need for the whispers.

I was miserable and lonely, but my son was alive. I was keeping him safe, *My Precious.*

· · · · · · ·

Turns out, children find ways to injure themselves. If you're a mother, you know this is true. My son looked at my corner-free pillow of a house and was like, "Okay. Challenge accepted!"

Ben was bruised from head to toe from jumping off furniture, climbing on countertops, swinging from closet bars. You name it, he tried it and had an injury from it. It was a full-time job keeping that kid in one piece.

At Ben's one-year checkup, the pediatrician asked me how I was adjusting to parenthood. I told him the truth: I was a frazzled mess. Exhausted from fighting against a child who was hell-bent on his own destruction. "I've covered every corner and softened every edge, but look! He's a walking bruise. There aren't enough pool noodles in the world to keep this kid safe!"

He laughed before realizing I was dead serious, then collected himself and sat down.

"I have this talk with every parent. I want you to know that, okay? Growing up is a process of discovering corners. You can't prevent every boo-boo. It's a parent's job to babyproof the house and buckle their children in correctly. You are doing that very well. But accidents happen, and Ben will get hurt. It's going to break your heart. Some lessons in life leave bruises, and that's okay. Pain is an important teacher."

• • • • • • •

Imagine you've been invited to a book club with all of your favorite friends. Childcare is provided and snacks will be free, and you are excited and ready to go. Adding to the intrigue of the whole affair, the title remains a secret. You are told it's a "best-selling, life-changing book," so you bring wine, ready to read. You hug your friends, find a comfortable chair, and wait for the big reveal. Then the hostess walks in and passes out the book. It's the King James Version of The Bible.

How do you feel looking down at your gift, sipping your glass of merlot? Are you frustrated? Angry? Do you feel you've been tricked? Are you cutting your eyes at your bestie on the couch, attempting to signal your horror? Two things: I'm sorry; I'm the one who invited you. And second, please stick around.

One of the hardest things a person can do is heal their perception of Scripture. Most of us have experienced seasons in life in which we've fallen out of love with the Bible. Maybe you are in such a season now. I've been there; I know how it happens.

So often, the Word is used as a weapon, wielding judgment and condemnation. As if there's no joy to be found in its pages, and it's only a collection of rules. And at our core, we know we are messy people. We *know* we fall short of God's law. The last thing we want is a browbeating, right? Some buzzkill collection of rules?

Don't eat too much. Don't lust after others. Don't let the sun go down on your anger. Don't be a drunkard. Don't gossip. Don't lie. Basically, don't do seven hundred things.

You can feel like a teenager, frustrated at Dad. All He does is ruin the fun!

As if God is some crummy father laid back in His heavenly La-Z-Boy, watching football and drinking a beer. Like He's mostly absent, unless your music's too loud, then he yells, *"Could you cut off that racket?!"*

Let me tell you, friend. That's not who God is. He created us in His own image. He wants us to know life at its fullest. He wants us to experience adventure, fall in love, and discover ourselves. He wants joy for His children, believe that. But the reality is this: Our world has plenty of sharp edges, and there are no pool noodles to soften our falls. God's a *good* Father, and He hates when we hurt. And that's why He gave us the Bible.

Have you ever been to the Tomorrowland Speedway at Disney World? It's my son's absolute favorite. Of course, I can't ride it without two Tylenol, and even then, I feel rickety afterward. There are guardrail-style bumpers built into the tracks, which keep each cart safe in its lane. I have the shakiest video of Ben behind the wheel, laughing hysterically as we swerved back and forth. The constant lurching creates legit whiplash, but you won't see a parent complain. Because we know the sheer chaos that would be unleashed on the world if those guardrails were suddenly gone. So we sit in the passenger seat and we laugh, because we love to witness our children's joy. Their souls are soaring, their feet heavy against the gas. The guardrails have given them wings.

• • • • • • •

My aunt Cindy offered to bring me to SeaWorld when I was five years old. Most of the family warned against this adventure, but Cindy was confident she could manage. When she picked me up for our special day, I am sure I looked like a cherub. My hair was pulled back in two adorable piggy tails; my pink dress had a whale stitched on the front. On my way out the door, Momma offered a leash that she used on me whenever we went through an airport. "A leash?" asked Cindy, laughing at the idea. "I'm sure we will be just fine!" Two hours later, my aunt blinked her eyes and I was nowhere to be seen. In a panic, she ran all around the park. As a mother now, I can't fathom her fear. The pit that formed in her stomach. Or the shock she felt when on the jumbo screen she saw a familiar, piggy-tailed child. I was a volunteer in the Shamu show, totally rocking that whale applique. Her niece was safe and happy as a clam. But what did my aunt Cindy feel?

I'm a mom now, so I think I can guess. My children know not to go near the street, we've discussed this rule ten thousand times. But once, my daughter beelined for the road, and of course a car was incoming. I raced to the sidewalk and snatched her to safety, feeling thrilled and relieved and furious. I wanted to kiss every inch of her unharmed body and shake her as hard as I could. In the end, I held her close and I cried.

"Why did you go near the road, baby? *Don't you remember our rules?*"

It seems to me that humans are born in a state of rebellion. From the moment we realize our autonomous will, we use it to challenge authority. We are toddlers who stick our fingers in light sockets. Teenagers who sneak out past curfew. We want to jump off the couch because it looks like fun. And honestly, sometimes it can be. There's this special shine, an air of intrigue, that surrounds anything off-limits. Since the Garden of Eden, creation has shown that we want the things we can't have. Sin wouldn't tempt us if it tasted sour the moment it touched our tongue. Ask Eve how tasty that apple was, right up 'til it ruined her life.

I believe this rebellion that's engrained in our souls can make a mess out of The Message. It gives us distaste for the Bible and the wisdom it contains. Nobody likes being told what to do, even if it's God who is telling us to do it. But therein lies the disconnect, and the problem with how we see Scripture. We are viewing the Bible as a collection of rules, when, in fact, it's our lifesaving guardrails. It's hard to see sometimes, but Scripture is there for our joy. Every "thou shalt" and "thou shalt not" is a track laid carefully in the ground. They aren't there for the sake of limiting our fun, but to keep us from descending into chaos.

The greatest king to rule over Israel was a man by the name of David. He is described in the Bible

> We are viewing the Bible as a collection of rules, when, in fact, it's our lifesaving guardrails.

as a "man after God's own heart." He's also one of the authors of Psalms. In Psalm 119:103, David praises the laws of God. He said, "How sweet are your words to my taste, sweeter than honey to my mouth!"

Now, I don't know about you, but I have never read the Ten Commandments and thought "Mmmmm, sure is decadent!" I would probably compare it to oatmeal with berries. It's good for me, and so I consume it.

But here's the thing: David had jumped the track of God's law on more than a few occasions. There was adultery, murder, and that whole messing up the Ark of the Covenant thing. He knew what it looked like to ignore God's Word and the pain that choice wrought in his life. He had sinned greatly and had suffered greatly and learned from those disasters. David relished the law and the freedom it gave him. He used God's Word as his protection—its boundaries were sweeter than honey.

• • • • • • •

I still have streaks of rebellion in my heart, little punk rock stripes of green. Perhaps they are lame compared to David's rap sheet, but still. I'm my own brand of rebel. I've had to work with a morning headache that was caused by "one more" martini (don't be a drunkard). I've had to make phone calls and apologize to friends for a snarky or heated remark (be slow to anger). I've gotten a ticket for driving 50 in a 35 (I knew I was driving too fast). I still skirt past those scriptural guardrails and bang my knee on the consequences.

And on those days, when my bad choices hurt...I ask myself, what if?

What if we stopped pushing past boundaries and instead appreciated them? What if we found gratitude for the safety they provide? Or how they show God's love for His kids?

I'm all about owning our whole life story, the hot holy mess that it is. But that doesn't mean that I fly off the rails and throw caution into the wind. The lie that we've been fed in this world is that total freedom is liberating. That when we indulge every whim, every desire in our heart, *that's* when we'll truly be happy. But history has shown our hearts to be liars. Remember your partying phase? That choice that hurt you, that job you lost, the fight you picked with your husband? *That* is the chaos unleashed in your world when the guardrails are suddenly gone. You chase what feels good, you finally get it, and you end up with a nasty bruise.

> What if we stopped pushing past boundaries and instead appreciated them?

So many times, when life gets hard, I think, *I hate growing up.* In childhood, there was no worrying about what I would eat, no bills that I had to pay. But more than that, I think it's because I was safe under Momma's rules. I knew too much sugar would make me sick. When to sleep so I wouldn't get grouchy. This is why children live their lives with the gas pedal pressed to the floorboard. Within their boundaries, they are safe and secure. The rules they follow are *liberating.*

Isn't that such a beautiful way to experience the Word of

God? I know I've said this, but it begs repeating: God's a good, good Father. He hates to see His children hurt, which is why He gave us the Bible. Not as a killjoy collection of rules, but a framework for experiencing freedom! David called God's Word "sweeter than honey"…you want to know something amazing? Honey is the only food on the planet that literally never goes bad. It is always sweet, always safe, and it magically preserves itself. If ever a perfect analogy existed, this might be the one.

It's taken time, but I'm moving on from my oatmeal and berries mentality. The Word of God is truly sweet, when received as the gift that it is. Look at your life, and you'll see it, too. The Bible is here for protection. For every destructive left turn you've taken—there is a scripture pointing to the right. The guardrails have always been there for our good.

If we trust them, they might give us wings.

CHAPTER 15

LIFE ON THE HAMSTER WHEEL

The world went and got itself in a big damn hurry.

—Brooks (in *Rita Hayworth and the Shawshank Redemption* by Stephen King)

I hate rats.

I'm guessing there aren't many people who particularly love rats, but it feels important to note that for the better part of my life, I tried very hard *not* to hate them. Because I am an animal lover through and through, something about blanket-hating an entire species felt at odds with that core value. So, for a while, I did my best to judge rats by their own individual merit. Like, Master Splinter, of Teenage Mutant Ninja Turtle fame. He was nice enough. And that subway rat that went viral for stealing a slice of pizza bigger than his body. He was relatable.

But ever since the Mr. Jingles incident, my deep, abiding hate for rats was dyed-in-the-wool. Perhaps this was due to the poor timing of our introduction, or the way he nibbled around his giblets looking for a flea to snack on. Whatever the case, that rat was the final freaking straw for me. The entire species is gross and beyond redemption.

Now hamsters, on the other hand…well, they're something altogether different. They are basically handheld teddy bears. They don't slum it in city sewers like their lowlife, ratty cousins. They don't eat trash pizza or spread the bubonic plague. No, hamsters just root around their wood shavings all day, looking perpetually adorable like the tiny corgis that they are.

My love affair with hamsters began around seventh grade, when Momma decided I should learn responsibility through pet ownership. Although I begged for a puppy, she preferred that I test my parenting skills on a rodent first. Lucky for us, Wet Pets was running a five-dollar hamster special that week. I remember strolling back and forth between the cages, studying the little critters. They were all so cute and fluffy. But after watching them interact for a while, I couldn't help but notice something: As precious as they were, hamsters were pretty much idiots.

In each cage there was a jingle ball, some colorful plastic tubing, and a wheel. And holy cow, did they fight over that wheel. The hamsters tumbled all over one another, just fighting for the chance to jump in and run their legs into a blur. That wheel would get moving at the speed of light, which is typically when their problems began. You see, their little biscuit bodies weren't cut out for sprinting, so after a few seconds of exertion, the hamsters would get tired and just…quit. But the wheel wouldn't quit.

It kept on turning. I watched in amazement as each hamster got sucked up by the momentum, like wet socks in the spin cycle. They would go round and round until the wheel would slow down and they'd come falling out, drunk from physics.

Eventually, I found my pet. He was an obese, ginger-colored hamster who spent his time hiding behind a purple tube. Whether he was self-aware or lazy, I didn't know, but he was the only hamster avoiding the spinny wheel, and I respected that. I named him Stuffing, handed over my five dollars, and brought him home.

Despite my feelings on the matter, the cage we purchased came with a complimentary hamster wheel. Momma helped me set it up, just in case. We figured, after a while, it might get boring living in a plastic box. If Stuffing wanted to take the wheel for a spin and burn off a little nervous energy, I wouldn't judge him for it (too much). He seemed to love his new home. He spent each day crawling through toilet paper tubes and pushing his little jingle ball around from corner to corner. He even learned to bathe himself under the bottle feeder. But not once did he ever jump inside the hamster wheel.

"Who is the smartest fluffer in the whole wide world?" I asked him every morning, while topping off the water bottle. Clearly, this question was rhetorical. Stuffing was the only hamster in the world that was smart enough to avoid the spin cycle. I picked him up to give him a little snuggle, and for the first time ever, Stuffing rolled over in my hand, exposing his adorable little pink feet. All *three* of them.

Horrified, I dropped Stuffing back into his cage. How did he lose a whole entire foot? Did it just...fall off? I grabbed a pencil and pushed around the wood shavings. But nope. Stuffing's foot was nowhere to be found.

I was devastated. Momma was not going to be impressed; how would I ever earn a puppy? And holy crap, if she knew there was a hamster foot lost somewhere in our house…

I ran downstairs, grabbed the phone, and called Wet Pets.

"Hi, this is Mary Katherine Samples. My family bought a hamster from your store three weeks ago, and I need to exchange it."

"Exchange it?"

"Yes, sir. It's missing a foot."

"Oh, I remember you. You bought that red Syrian hamster?"

"Yes, that's me."

The voice on the other line paused for a moment, and I could've sworn I heard a chuckle.

"Ma'am, you bought him with three feet."

"Wait. I did?"

"Yes…we thought that's why you liked him."

I politely got off the phone and ran upstairs to my room. Stuffing was there, chugging his water, happy as a clam. I leaned over the cage to scratch his back, but he skittered away to his toilet paper roll. There was a little hitch in his gait that suddenly seemed very obvious.

Oh, I thought. *That explains a lot.*

It turned out, Stuffing wasn't the smartest fluffer in the world, after all. He was just an ordinary hamster with a missing foot who instinctually knew that the wheel was a bad idea.

Either way, he'd avoided the spin cycle.

• • • • • • •

"We have fourteen dollars until my next shift," I said as I poured myself a cup of coffee.

In our second year of marriage, Ian and I had come to understand that love wasn't enough for *everything*. Our anniversary was two days away, and Ian had asked if a dinner date was something we could afford. He was in medical school, and I was a waitress at a local barbecue joint, so things in the Backstrom family were usually pretty tight. The balance in our bank account rarely surpassed double digits. This week would not be the exception.

"No big deal," he said, kissing me on the cheek. "We can do a picnic instead."

He headed out the door for a gross anatomy lab, and I sat down to finish my coffee. We would figure something out; we always did. But there weren't any shifts for me to pick up, so that meant I'd have to get creative. I chugged the rest of my coffee and spotted a Bible nearby, sitting atop a pile of bills. I reached across the table and grabbed it.

Maybe Jesus will have some truth.

I opened the Bible to a random page and couldn't believe my eyes. Folded in half and tucked neatly in the Psalms was a worn twenty-dollar bill. It wasn't a lot, but it gave us margin. I said a prayer of gratitude and opened a Google tab. The budget for our anniversary had more than doubled, and I couldn't wait to surprise my husband.

When Saturday arrived, I told Ian to wear his favorite polo shirt. That was our version of fancy back then.

"We have big plans, mister," I said with a wink. Ian raised an eyebrow.

"Um, should I be scared?"

"That depends," I laughed. "Have you ever been to the dollar movie?"

I'd managed to find a place on the outskirts of town with a five o'clock showing of *The Bourne Ultimatum*. At typical theaters, the price of two tickets would swallow our weekly grocery budget. This was the only way we could afford to go, and I was giddy to have an adventure.

"The reviews recommend not drinking anything before the movie. I guess the bathrooms are a little questionable."

"Meaning...?"

"Oh, nothing crazy. Missing stall doors, sticky floors, that sort of thing. As long as we don't have to pee, we should be fine."

"Sounds reasonable," he replied. "Let's go."

I hid two baggies of candy in my purse, and the usher totally busted me. I guess he was looking for something more nefarious than contraband Skittles, because he closed my bag and shooed us along.

"Theater four on the right," he said. "There's not a number, but it's right past theater two."

Ian and I took our seats and cackled like children when they creaked beneath our weight. The movie reel had spots all over it, and the speaker system cracked quite a bit—but we didn't care. I weaved my arm around his elbow and snuggled in close for the movie. About thirty minutes shy of the end, I got a little wiggly.

"Babe?" I whispered.

"Yes?" he replied.

"I have to pee."

We ended up at Wendy's a little earlier than I planned, but I was grateful for a clean bathroom and a stall with a door attached. Ian poked fun at my peanut-sized bladder, but the truth was, he didn't mind leaving. There was a table for two in the corner of the restaurant, with a dusty fake flower in a plastic vase. Ian pulled out my chair and asked what I wanted from the extra value menu. We raised our Frostys for a toast and spent the rest of the evening wondering aloud how different life would eventually become.

When we'd have kids. When we'd have jobs. When we'd have more than fourteen dollars to our name.

· · · · · · ·

When I was a kid, I couldn't wait to be a full-fledged adult. I wanted the latitude that came with maturity, and I couldn't wait to call my own shots. There would be dessert for dinner, nonexistent bedtimes, and the ability to buy whatever toy I wanted. It was going to be great.

When I was in college, I dreamed of life as a married woman. I couldn't wait to share every day until forever with the love of my life. He'd rub my shoulders as I scrambled eggs, and we'd make the cutest babies. Our children would say *yes, ma'am* and *no, thank you* and brush their teeth without being told.

These flash-forward "memories" set many expectations for how my life would play out over time. And perhaps it goes without saying, but as each of these milestones were realized, my life looked nothing like I imagined it would.

I wonder what it is about human beings that we spend so much of our very short existence wishing time away. Do we think at some point our struggles will disappear, and nothing will rise up to replace them?

Is this a modern problem? An American problem? A millennial problem?

A couple days ago, I was reading Exodus, and my Writer Eyeballs spotted something that didn't make any freaking sense. It was chapter 24, verse 12, but only the first half of the verse spoke to me.

> *And the Lord said unto Moses, Come up to me into the mount, and be there.*
>
> —Exodus 24:12 KJV

I know, this seems like a strange thing to be fixated on, but here's the thing, y'all: If I wrote that line and sent it off to my editor, she would respond and say, "Hey, MK. This part right here is a bit repetitive. You've already told Moses to come up to the mount. It isn't necessary to follow up with 'and be there.'"

But this wasn't just any bit of Scripture, it was a "thus sayeth" scenario, straight from the mouth of God. There had to be a reason for that redundancy, I just knew it. So, I went online and started digging into the original language, into the commentaries of biblical scholars—anything I could find to explain why God would speak in such a peculiar way. And while I unearthed four different theories, all intelligently formed, there was one in particular that sang to my spirit. It went something like this: God had something big planned for Moses, and He didn't want him showing up to Mt. Sinai distracted. He wanted Moses to set aside his stress, his worry, and the challenges of life in the valley. To be there: quiet, intentional, and waiting for the Lord.

It didn't make sense to me at first, but it became profoundly meaningful to me.

"Come up to the mountain and be there," said the Lord. If a man like Moses required this reminder, what did that mean for a person like me?

· · · · · · ·

Ten years after our dollar movie date, Ian and I sat down for a five-star dinner in Manhattan. His polo shirt was not invited; reservations required a tie. We sat in silence for the first thirty minutes, sipping craft cocktails and considering appetizers. Ian had been a doctor for two whole years, and our lives had drastically changed in that time.

"The oysters Rockefeller sounds good," he said.

"I think we should try the gnocchi," I replied.

"We get gnocchi at our favorite restaurant home. Let's try the oysters."

"Oysters are better in Florida," I said.

The waiter came and took our order. We both got salads, instead.

After a minute of silent tension, I finished my martini.

"Are you happy?" I blurted out, yanking the top off a whole can of worms.

Ian didn't answer, but instead twirled his glass in a circle, making a tiny whirlpool with the ice. The air between us felt thick and loaded.

"Not really," he finally replied. "I'm honestly pretty miserable."

Fourteen years into our relationship, we had claimed our American dream: a beautiful home, two golden retrievers, and cars that didn't rattle on the interstate. We had two healthy children and a circle of support to help raise them. After years of constant financial stress, it blew me away that we were having this conversation. In this moment, in New York City. With these stupid, overpriced salads. We had everything we'd ever wanted, and we were unhappy as we'd ever been.

I remembered that night in the Wendy's dining room, and how everything felt so light back then. How a plastic flower and a cup of chili was more than enough to say grace over. How Ian and I laughed like children in a dank, run-down theater. We never even finished the movie, but it didn't matter. Where did we go wrong?

I listened as Ian unloaded his heart, and I waited to respond in kind. Listening to one another talk, it was clear that a fracture had occurred. Over time, the contentment we had in our circumstances was replaced by an insatiable need to reach a little bit higher.

Not just a family home, a historic family home.

Not a job at any hospital, the one that pays the most.

Not a vacation for the sake of rest, but a vacation that made us feel better about how much time Ian had to spend at work.

After all, Ian worked hard so we could have nice things—and nice things were fun to have. So, he'd buckle down and work more shifts, but that would make him tired. Then, we'd raise our lifestyle. Because hardworking folks deserve to feel rewarded, right?

Work hard, play hard, work hard, play hard. It was a cycle that always demanded more. Ian and I had bought into the lie that things of this world could give us joy. We'd jumped on that wheel with our whole entire hearts and run until our legs were tired. In the end, we got caught in the spin cycle. And on our twelfth anniversary, we were spit out of the machine, feeling drunk and disoriented from the physics of it all. Just like those idiot hamsters.

· · · · · · ·

The day I adopted Stuffing, I left Wet Pets with an uneasy feeling. I felt like somebody should tell the hamsters. Not only how ridiculous they looked, but how much energy they were wasting in the process.

Sometimes, I wonder what God is thinking, watching us here on earth. Does He feel the horror I felt that day, strolling the aisles at Wet Pets? Does He shake His head as we fight over a wheel that goes absolutely nowhere?

The thing is, God created us with intrinsic human desires. He also gave us the ability to satisfy those desires. We get hungry, and food is a thing. We get aroused, and sex is a thing. Unfortunately, sin is also a thing.

This means we can have normal, godly desires but go haywire in our attempts to satisfy them. A desire to eat can give way to gluttony. A desire for sex can give way to adultery. Desire itself isn't a fault of design; it's our pursuit of satisfaction that causes us trouble.

There's a holy ache in each of our souls that spurs us toward our purpose. It's human nature to reach a little higher, to long for adventure, to want to achieve. But the guardrails are written all throughout Scripture on how to satisfy that ache. And never, not even once, does the Bible suggest that things of this world would do the trick.

● ● ● ● ● ● ●

If you're wondering whether or not you're on the hamster wheel, there's a couple of ways that you can tell. First up is that soul-deep restlessness. An unshakable feeling that there's got to be more, even when you're trying your hardest. You're accomplishing the things you've always sworn you'd do, volunteering in your spare time, working out. You feel driven to keep going, going, going... but there's no sense of progress or purpose. Your mind keeps wandering during those endless spins...Is this all there is?

If you want to feel peace, if you want to feel purpose, you have to stay off the dang hamster wheel.

Another way to tell is that chronic fatigue. I'm not talking about some physical symptom. This is a soul-deep exhaustion. You wake up tired, and you go to bed tired, but sleep doesn't replenish your battery.

You'd like to pull yourself out of this funk, but that'd require way too much energy.

If you want to feel peace, if you want to feel purpose, you have to stay off the dang hamster wheel. Assuming that's what you want for your life, ask yourself: *What's got me spinning?* For my family, it was centering our life around money. The collecting of earthly possessions. For yours, it might be something else entirely. It's easy to locate the problem. That place in life that sends stress levels soaring? That fills your head up with noise? Those are the things that are making you crazy. It's time to start cutting them out.

· · · · · · ·

When Ian and I got home from that New York dinner date, my husband cut back his hours at work. We moved out of our big, fancy house and rented a cottage in a neighborhood nearby. We stopped relying so heavily on babysitters and spent more time in the trenches of parenthood. We stopped investing money in treasures on earth and tried harder to invest in each other. Over the past year, a flood of change has been roaring through my family. And while I have no idea where its current will take us, I believe it is someplace better.

But I can tell you this: In this season of change, the joy has returned to my marriage. We find ourselves laughing a whole lot more. We hear one another more clearly. We have cut out the noise and quieted our hearts. We are listening for God's holy whispers.

And listen, I know I don't have the holy credentials of Moses. But still, I lean into those peculiar words spoken to him in Exodus.

I'm stepping off this hamster wheel and showing up to the mountain. For a while, I'm just going to *be here*. Quiet. Intentional. And waiting to hear from the Lord.

CHAPTER 16

THE MESSINESS WAS THE POINT

In my dream, the angel shrugged & said, If we fail this
time, it will be a failure of imagination & then she
placed the world gently in the palm of my hand.

—Brian Andreas

When I first set out to write this book, I had one hope for
you, friend: that as we journeyed together, one page at
a time, you'd see glimpses of God in the mess. Not some magnificent unveiling of His purpose for us, but a forensic dusting
for fingerprints. Evidence that God has His hands on our lives,
piecing the puzzle together.

I wish I could offer some revolutionary path that would
allow you to sidestep your struggles. "The Secret to a Mess-Free
Life," or something—a Bible study *with* a juice cleanse! I could

write that book, and fill it with platitudes, and maybe Oprah would put it in her book club. But the reality is this: The world will continue to remain broken, and in it, we'll experience mess.

Yesterday, I found myself laughing at the fact that the poop emoji is in my "most used" list. Lately, when friends text and ask how I'm doing, my response has mostly been: *crap*. For context, I'm writing this book in 2020. The mess is more oppressive than funny these days. There's a pandemic, which is its own special brand of horrible. Now I'm homeschooling kids while working from home, which is like brushing your teeth while eating Oreos. On a national scale, our politics have been playing out like an episode of *Maury*. So, I think it's valid that a smiley-faced swirl of poo has made its way into my daily jargon.

A few months ago, my editor reached out and said, "MK, we are noticing a pattern. You are writing a lot of stories from childhood, and not as many from your current life." I sat down to ponder why that was, and the answer I came up with was this: Time allows us a bird's-eye view on the work God has done in our life. That devastating high school breakup makes a lot more sense when you've been married for fourteen years. But if you asked me at sixteen years old to dig deep in that pain and share the words in my heart? I think the best I could muster in that moment of mess would be a verbal little brown swirl: *crap*.

The dusting for fingerprints comes after the fact; right now, we just have to get through it. We are active construction sites, chaos and mud. But God has a blueprint for all of it. He can make purpose of pain, and meaning from chaos, if—

if, if, if—we let go and trust Him to do it.

Something strange happened today: God spoke to me at a traffic light.

It was odd timing, for sure. But that's how God operates. I can fast for two days, read my Bible every night, go to church six times a week. Nothing. I can keep my mind and spirit silent and pray for some answers to come. Nothing.

Then, I'm stuck at a red light, of all stinking places, my daughter thrashing around in her car seat. And it's in *that* moment, through her blood-curdling screams, that I hear a familiar whisper.

Let me unpack this scenario further, because the absurdity has to be shared. My four-year-old daughter was having this meltdown over a freaking paper clip. One of her friends had apparently given it to her during preschool, and she was so excited she snuck it home in her clothes. But as I was driving, the magical paper clip fell out of her clothes and into the abyss that is my car's filthy floorboard. Then, despite her desperate pleas, I refused to pull over so she could unbuckle and find it.

This made my daughter *big* mad. I'm talking wailing and gnashing of teeth.

"You are an *evil* mommy! A wicked stepmother! I wish I had a better mommy!"

Un-freaking-believable, right? I gave birth to that little turdlet, and she had the audacity to disown me over a paper clip. So, I let her mourn and scream. There was no reasoning with her, anyways. A heart wants what it wants. To Holland, that paper clip was the most valuable thing she'd ever owned. But I couldn't stop thinking…

If only she knew what was coming. If she knew why I wouldn't pull over. If she knew I was hurrying to take her for ice cream, just the two of us, before soccer practice. She would be thrilled.

There was something in store for my daughter that was so much better than a few inches of twisted wire. But that paper clip was her heart's desire, and beyond it she could see nothing else. I was contemplating how ridiculous this was when God smacked me upside the head.

Are you listening, MK? You are this toddler.

And holy cow, y'all. It all made sense. I'm just a child, stuck in a car seat, clutching my precious paper clips. I should be excited that God is taking me somewhere, just the two of us, but I can't see past my own wants.

· · · · · · ·

My writing job changes, but I liked my job.

A speaking gig falls between my fingers, but it's the one I was most excited about.

My husband changes as a human, but I was comfortable with who he was.

It's the letting go part that we struggle with, right? The trusting God in the process. I've just written an entire book about my mess and how God's fingerprints were in all of it—but ask me where He is in my life *right now*. In the places the mud is fresh and my broken edges are raw. In the pandemic and politics and the stress in my family. In my perpetual mental health struggles. Where are the fingerprints of God in that? Honestly, *I don't know*.

The truth is, I struggle with trusting God, too. I hate it when

I'm not in control. Even when He's shown me again and again that He's working in my life for good, I find myself angry, and pitching a fit. *This wasn't the life I had planned!*

"My paper clips, God! Pull over and let me collect them! *Pull over, God—Waaaaaaah!*"

All the while, He is waiting for the wailing to stop, so we can hear him say, "*My child.* Stop crying, and trust your Father. There's something far better ahead."

I know it can feel like you're stuck in one place, with your paper clips all over the floorboard. It is hard to hear truth in the midst of the mess. We're distracted, and too busy wailing. But God wants hot fudge sundaes and sprinkles for us. His plans for You are good. The purpose of your life is so much bigger than your messes would have you believe.

> The purpose of your life is so much bigger than your messes would have you believe.

• • • • • • •

I always get tickled when people believe they are too messy to be a "real Christian." Sure, your sailor mouth might get the side-eye at First Baptist, but you think Jesus is clutching His pearls? "Well, that's it. I was really rooting for that daughter of mine, but she stubbed her toe and an f-bomb flew out!"

Let me break it to you, friend: Your rap sheet isn't impressive enough to break grace. There's no mind too dirty, no past too shady, that it can scare Jesus away. His death on the cross covered it all, so you could walk away clean. That five hundred dollars you hid under the Monopoly board one time when you were ten? Covered. Last week, when you lied about your weight to the doctor? Covered. And not just the everyday, Little League stuff—those things we admit to and giggle. There's lying, addiction, adultery, murder. All of it. By His grace, covered.

Women like to poke fun at ourselves for our lives being hot messes. We find solidarity in owning up to our relatable, rough edges. That's why there are so many popular bloggers with mom buns and trashed-out minivans. There's a particular level of mess that plays well to the masses, earning a badge of "realness." We are sympathetic to that sitcom brand of chaos, but beyond that...things get weird.

God forbid your mess look like a divorce, poverty, or severe depression. Maybe you struggle with alcoholism. That doesn't play well on a blog. We like imperfection in tiny doses, because we think that makes us human. But the truth is, behind every messy bun, there's a woman who needs time for herself. Behind the wheel of that trashed-out van is a frazzled, exhausted mother. Stress creates mess creates stress creates mess, and it's not always dosed out in teaspoons. So what do we do when it's all overwhelming? Do we hand it to God? Or hide?

When my kids were potty training, they'd crap their pants while hiding behind a curtain. They would do this deed just two feet away, like I didn't know what was happening. Then, with dumps like a truck, they'd waddle out of hiding and ask me for assistance. Hiding from Momma is pretty ridiculous when, ultimately, I'm cleaning the mess.

And yet, who am I to judge my kid? I regularly hide from God. When my depression is heavy, or my marriage is cracking, or I feel shame from my addiction to food. Do I run to the arms of my loving Father? No, I go find a curtain. I don't want anyone to see me like this. I mean, this is real mess. It's not cute or relatable. I'm ashamed. *Look over there, God!*

My friend, please hear me in this. Because it will save you (and me) so much hurt. It's absurd to pretend that crap isn't happening when, clearly, it's filled up our pants. There is no need to hide from the gaze of our Father. He has called us to grace, as-is. This is a fully-informed-of-the-crap kind of love. God knows what you have in your britches.

· · · · · · ·

If my husband were a Disney princess, he would be Moana.

I've never seen a person who relishes the sea quite like Ian does. At the crack of dawn, he will paddle out on his surfboard and bob like a buoy for hours. In the sea, his soul finds some bit of rest. It's a place where he can recharge his batteries. Now, this isn't his book, so I won't share the details of Ian's personal messes. But I can tell you he has them, because all of us do. And sometimes, they swallow him whole. And it's in those times, when the world feels heavy, that Ian longs for the sea. It's not my thing, but I do understand it. Everyone has their place.

Maybe yours is on the back of a horse, near a mountain, or by the lake. You know, that place where you find your own rhythm, and the outside world falls away. We have a soul-deep need to escape sometimes. We long for a hideaway place. It's an instinctual thing that we've known since childhood, building our first blanket forts. These are the places I'm talking about. When you are there, everything's safe. Or at least that's the illusion we are buying in to. We want to suspend disbelief.

When Ian returns from his surfing trips, there's a period of time when he's bluesy. It's almost as if he'd rather not have gone and tasted that world of reprieve. Life hits you hard when you're back from vacation, and your mess is right where you left it.

Reality is, the ocean is peaceful, but it can't wash away student debt. The mountains are gorgeous and worthy of awe, but they can't repair a strained marriage. Yet, again and again, we return to these places, expecting to find lasting peace.

I think, deep down, every one of us knows there are itches this world can't quite scratch. We resent that truth most in the moments that follow the days we capture the carrot. We get the promotion we always wanted, but it turns out that it still feels like work. The Costa Rican vacation was amazing, but now we're back home in the suburbs. The carrot is gone, and it left us hungry. So, we immediately replace it with an apple. We plan a new trip in a shinier city. We grasp the next step on the ladder. And if we get that apple, will we be satisfied? Or will that hunger remain unsatiated?

Okay, MK. I think I hear you. You say I should quit chasing joy. That nothing on earth will ever make me happy, and beach trips are making it worse?

I promise, dear reader, that's not where we're going. I love C. S. Lewis, not Friedrich Nietzsche. I believe there is pleasure in this world, but I know that it won't fill us up. What I'm saying is this: Every deep desire, every ache in your soul, is an arrow that points to your Father. It shows us the absence of what we need most.

It's the God-shaped hole in our lives. Or, in the words of C. S. Lewis: "If we find ourselves with a desire that nothing in this world can satisfy, the most probable explanation is that we were made for another world."

A few years ago, I paid a visit to the Smithsonian National Museum of Natural History. After casually perusing the current exhibits, I discovered the Hall of Fossils. I was awestruck by how much archaeologists learn by holes left in the ground. My favorite fossil

C. S. Lewis: "If we find ourselves with a desire that nothing in this world can satisfy, the most probable explanation is that we were made for another world."

was a dragonfly mold; it looked like a perfect stamp. Just a negative impression of a once-living thing, preserved in ancient stone. The mere outline of that dragonfly painted a detailed picture in my mind. It was purple and green, with silvery wings. Nearly the size of my hand. When I closed my eyes, I could almost see it wake up and flutter away.

• • • • • • •

You and I have come so far together. We are practically fellow goat thieves now. Assuming we can be one hundred percent honest, I have one last confession to make:

I am still a holy hot mess. I don't know if that's going to change. I still yell at my children; I still fight with my husband; I still eat packages of Oreos when I'm sad. In my heart I know that the things of this world will leave me wanting more. In my heart I know that there's a God-shaped hole that He alone can satisfy. But in my brain? I wouldn't mind a shiny gold NYT BEST SELLER sticker on the cover of this book. I would love to lose about fifty pounds and buy a house on top of a mountain. I'm not proud of my mess, but I can't fake perfect. I'm a bad liar and an even worse actress. But there's a weightier reason I share my stories without smoothing the rough edges out. And it's the reason I ask you to do the same thing:

Be honest about the mess.

One of my favorite movies from childhood is *Rudolph the Red-Nosed Reindeer and the Island of Misfit Toys*. If you weren't blessed with the privilege of watching this classic, I'll tell you right now: It's odd. There's a bad guy named Mr. Cuddles, who is kidnapping toys so children will never outgrow them. There's a blimp involved, and a hippopotamus queen, and Rudolph is considering a nose job. Against this backdrop, Rudolph and friends arrive at this misfit island, where they meet a cast of quirky toys, sequestered away in their shame. There's a Charlie-in-the-Box, a bird that swims, a cowboy who rides an ostrich. And as an introduction to their community, the toys break out in song. They reveal each attribute that, in their own minds, gives them oddball status: There's a spotted elephant, a choo choo with square wheels, and a water pistol that shoots jelly. Together, they bemoan their quirks through song and proclaim: "We're all misfits!" I think this part was supposed to be sad, but I totally missed that memo. A happy little island of honest misfits sounded like heaven to me. Can you imagine belonging to a community like that? Those who wouldn't bother hiding their weird?

Oh, you're a bird that swims in water? Well, yee-haw! I ride an ostrich! You feel weird about your polka-dot skin? Well, check out my square wheels!

On what planet would this be considered exile? These misfits have found their people! A truer tragedy would be faking perfect, hiding your spots, and trying to conform. The misfit toys have created a haven, and it's what I pray you discover. That by showing up each day, boldly broken, your very own little island might form.

You'd find a church that, on Sunday mornings, welcomes your Saturday mess. You'd find your fellow goat thieves, who love and adore you for the ostrich-riding cowgirl you are. You'd come to God with your polka dots showing, because that is the point, after all.

Your life is the backdrop of God's greatest miracles. Your mess is the clay in His hands. And believe me, friend, when our God is moving, He's going to leave an impression. The stamp of His presence pressed deep in your life is the outline of who He is. By sharing your story, you are sharing the gospel. Don't you dare water it down. How beautiful that God has embraced our worst and presented it as His best. He loves us, adores us, and has a plan for us.

We are *holy* in our hot mess.

ACKNOWLEDGMENTS

There are so many people who helped bring this book to life, and to whom I am forever indebted. To each of you, "thank you" feels grossly insufficient. But I searched the thesaurus and there's nothing better. I suppose it will have to do.

I must start by thanking my agent, Mike Salisbury. You are the ninja assassin in my corner. Thank you for believing in me, for answering so many manic phone calls, and for introducing me to Jeni's Splendid Ice Creams. I used to wonder why authors thanked their agents first. I don't wonder about that anymore.

To Karen, Curtis, and Sealy: Thank you for betting on a wildcard writer. I am so proud to be a part of the Yates and Yates family. I am sticking to y'all like a cat on a curtain. Hope you're happy about it.

Karen Longino. *Ma'am.* I don't even know what to say. If you have regretted giving me your cell phone number, you never once acted like it. Thank you for so many things. For Mom Babble. For my first "big girl" book deal. For being an actual friend. You are so, so dear to me.

Julie Lyles Carr. You jumped into a hot mess manuscript with so much optimism and care. Thank you for treating my words like your very own baby, for living inside my brain, and for extracting treasure from the abyss. You are a literary archaeologist. Please work with me forever.

ACKNOWLEDGMENTS

Thank you to the staff of Cristoff's and Waffle House, where *Holy Hot Mess* was written. Especially Shannon, Christian, and Cynthia, who always treated me like family. Your friendship, support, and incredible hospitality got me through this, chapter by chapter.

Now for the people who, for some crazy reason, stay in my life without any compensation. My friends and family…

Thank you, Ian, for supporting my every endeavor—except for the FBI thing, which was totally fair. You fight so hard for our family's happiness; our joy is your everlasting credit. I love you, B. Thank you for choosing me fifteen years ago, and for choosing me every day since.

To my children, Ben and Holland: I love you so much. You fill these pages and my heart with laughter. You two are my life's greatest joy.

Thank you, Mama (who recently told me that I spell *momma* wrong). You've invested thirty-seven years (and counting) in my mess: from potty training to cleaning up spilled milk to wiping away my tears. Thank you for being my safe place, always. I love you, *Momma*. (See, I *do* listen.)

Thank you, Joe Joe, who signed up for this madness. You made our family whole.

Thank you, Daddy, for answering my calls (no matter what hour they came). For being gentle as I passionately argue my politics, and for allowing me space to grow. And DD, for your steadfast spirit and bleeding heart. You came into our family right on time.

Thank you to my siblings: Karen Leigh, Ty, Justin, and Jackson. Each of you has loved me through different phases of mess.

Thank you for supporting me, for tolerating my seasonal shenanigans, and for being my built-in best friends. Don't forget that I have dirt on all of you.

To Addie, Birdie, Elijah, and Wyatt (and any second gens yet to come): Stay wild, laugh loud, and never grow up. Remember, Aunt Critter is here for you when things get messy.

To Kurt, Suzi, Ben, and Judi: Team Backstrom has never let me down. I am so proud to be a part of this family. Thank you for loving me well.

To Eliot, my sounding board and backup husband, and to Melissa, who finally admitted she loves me: Thank you for loving the Backstroms so well that our children "want to be Gold-en-ers."

To Mer Mer and Sara, my wolfpack: I could spend so many words on how much I love us, but the best thing is, y'all already know. As soon as we have our rabies shots, let's go get naps, fancy ramen, and Broadway.

Amy, my person: You are such a giver. And I'm not talking about the "I Pooped on Purpose" coffee mug or the John Krasinski face earrings. Your friendship is the best gift you've given me, and I won't apologize for being cheesy about it.

The Blanket Fort: My hideaway from the rest of the world. Thank you for your kindness and support, and for always making me laugh. #OGHamstersForLife

And last but never least: Thank you, dear reader. For picking up this book and journeying with me. I love each and every one of you hot, holy messes.

I hope you found joy in each page.

SCRIPTURE CREDITS

Scripture quotations marked (KJV) are taken from the King James Version of the Holy Bible.

ABOUT THE AUTHOR

Mary Katherine Backstrom is an award-winning author and influencer, best known for her viral videos and candid writing on family, faith, and mental illness. She has been featured on *Today Show* and CNN, and in the *New York Times*—but her friends and family are most impressed with her one-time appearance on *Ellen*. MK resides in Alabama with her husband, children, two dogs, and a cat. When she isn't writing, MK is active in her church, her community, and her favorite Mexican restaurant.